THE GERMAN UNIVERSITY

Daniel Fallon

THE GERMAN UNIVERSITY

A Heroic Ideal
in Conflict with
the Modern World

COLORADO ASSOCIATED UNIVERSITY PRESS

Copyright © 1980 by Daniel Fallon
Published by Colorado Associated University Press
Boulder, Colorado 80309
ISBN 0-87081-088-X
Library of Congress Catalog Card Number 80-66184
Printed in the United States of America

Publication of this book was made possible, in part,
by a grant from the Eugene M. Kayden Memorial
Fund.

For Carlos, Maureen, and Patty

Contents

O alte Burschenherrlichkeit,
Wohin bist du verschwunden?
Nie kehrst du wieder, goldne Zeit,
So froh und ungebunden!
Vergebens spähe ich umher,
Ich finde deine Spur nicht mehr,
O jerum, jerum, jerum,
O quae mutatio rerum!

—Eugen Höfling (1808-1880)

PREFACE

In 1959 I began a year as part of my undergraduate student experience that would include six months' employment as a social worker in Wuppertal and five months as a student at the University of Tübingen. I found the German university not only important and mysterious, but highly resistant to attempts to understand it. Its history, structure, and functions seemed no place to be collected conveniently. I was able to piece together what I needed for my own personal understanding from many different sources.

When I returned to Germany as a professor in 1973 for another year, I had in mind the possibility of a short article on the then current struggle for reform and transformation within the German university. Remembering my own frustration earlier, I realized that an English-speaking audience would have difficulty understanding such an article without some broader background material. The article thus grew backward to include a brief but accurate basis for understanding the university. Then, as reform moved toward a kind of closure in the decade of the 1970s, the article grew forward as well. Eventually my article turned into this small book.

I am responsible for all translations from German used in this essay. Most of the research was accomplished in 1973-74 during my tenure as a Senior Fulbright-Hays Research Fellow and as Visiting Professor of Psychology at the University of Düsseldorf, while I was on sabbatical leave from the State University of New York at Binghamton. I am grateful to Professors G. A. Lienert and W. Janke for their invitation to the Psychological Institute at Düsseldorf, and to the Fulbright Commission for its support. The material collected in the library of the *Westdeutsche Rektorenkonferenz* in Bonn proved invaluable; I thank the chief librarian, C. Stribrny, for her skilled and friendly cooperation.

Finally, I am deeply indebted to Antioch College and to Paul and Gertrud Hopf for teaching me the German language and introducing me to the culture of Germany.

Translation of the epigraph. At the beginning of this book there appears the first stanza of a poem composed by a German student during the flowering of the German university in the nineteenth century. This popular poem was taken up as a drinking song in university towns, a song that is still heard often today. The first stanza can be roughly translated as follows:

O glory of those grand old student days,
Where have you gone away?
You'll never come back, you golden time,
So happy, free of care!
In vain I look around me,
I've lost all trace of you,
O jerum, jerum, jerum,
How the world does change!

ONE
INTRODUCTION

The diversity of institutions in central Europe that is called collectively the German university has provided one of the more successful models of higher education since universities began to develop in the middle ages. The influence of the German university on American higher education, particularly on the U.S. graduate school, has been profound. Many of Charles W. Eliot's comprehensive and trend-setting curricular reforms at Harvard during the latter part of the nineteenth century, including effective advocacy of the free-elective system, can be traced to the influence of the German model and perhaps more directly to a seminal sojourn he took in Germany shortly before assuming the presidency of Harvard. The Johns Hopkins University, the University of Michigan, and the University of Chicago are just a few prominent examples of several institutions initially founded with the German model explicitly in mind.

The University of Michigan, for example, was chartered in Detroit in 1817 with a rationale heavily influenced by Napoleonic ideals. However, a "Prussian" influence was brought to bear in 1835 when General I. E. Crary, chairman of the education committee in the Michigan Constitutional Convention, and J. D. Pierce, Superintendent of Public Instruction, sought to apply principles from Victor Cousin's *Report on the State of Public Instruction in Prussia,* a document intended for the Ministry of Public Instruction in France, to the new state of Michigan. When Michigan was admitted to statehood in 1837, the university was moved from Detroit to Ann Arbor, but it was not until 1852 that the first president of the University of Michigan, Henry Philip Tappan, was appointed. A devotee of German higher education, he went to Ann Arbor directly upon returning from a period of study in Europe, and in the 1853-4 University of Michigan catalog he wrote, "The system of public instruction adopted by the State of Michigan is copied from the Prussian, acknowledged to be the most perfect in the world . . ." Although Tappan fought vigorously to establish graduate faculties and seminars on the German model, and made real progress toward this goal, he was unceremoniously relieved in 1863 by an unsympathetic board of regents, who favored a less pretentious and more practical university. Because of this and similar failures, it is usually argued that the U.S. graduate school, and with it the full implantation of the German model in America, did not arrive until the founding of The Johns Hopkins University in 1876.[1]

In 1891, G. Stanley Hall, founder of the American Psychological Association and president of Clark University, another institution formed on the German model, maintained that

> The German University is today the freest spot on earth. . . . Never was such burning and curiosity. . . . Shallow, bad ideas have died and truth has always attained power. . . . Nowhere has the passion to push on to the

frontier of human knowledge been so general. Never have so many men stood so close to nature and history or striven with such reverence to think God's thoughts after Him exactly.[2]

Forty years later, and well after the First World War, Abraham Flexner, founding force and first director of the Institute for Advanced Study at Princeton, commented in a similar vein:

> The German university has for almost a century and a half fruitfully engaged in teaching and research. As long as those two tasks combine in fertile union, the German university, whatever its defects of detail, will retain its importance. It has stimulated university development in Great Britain; from it has sprung the graduate school of the new world; to it industry and health and every conceivable practical activity are infinitely indebted.[3]

Another forty years later, and after another world war, the German university no longer commanded the respect it was once so richly tendered. James B. Conant, former president of Harvard University, and former ambassador to the Federal Republic of Germany, referred in exasperation to the German university in 1964 as "the best in the world—for the nineteenth century."[4] Clark Kerr, former president of the University of California, as president of the Carnegie Commission on Higher Education proposed eight tests for the evaluation of national systems of higher education and then used them to assess educational systems in nine large nations. The Federal Republic of Germany was considered strong on none of these tests, and was considered particularly weak on two.[5]

What is the state of the university in the Federal Republic of Germany today? What happened to the model that inspired so many thoughtful scholars? How can the past of the German university be reconciled with its present or its future? These are some of the questions which prompted the present inquiry. In hopes of offering insight to formulate answers for such questions, I have attempted to describe the contemporary university within the Federal Republic of Germany* in the context of its past.[6] The point of departure is the founding of the University of Berlin in 1810 because the central idea of the German university, even today, is rooted deeply in this pivotal event.

---

*Only universities in the Federal Republic of Germany, for which the historical continuity with the influential "Humboldtian" university is clear, are considered here. Universities in Austria and Switzerland are somewhat similar, but differ significantly in their historical development. Universities in the German Democratic Republic occasionally claim to be the true heirs of the Humboldt tradition, and it may be true that they have preserved more of the old customs than their Western counterparts. However, the course of their development has been sufficiently different from universities in the Federal Republic to warrant separate treatment, which is beyond the scope of this essay.

TWO
MOVEMENT TOWARD A NEW UNIVERSITY:
BERLIN, PRUSSIA, 1808

Perhaps the most remarkable fact about the widely admired German university of the nineteenth century is that it had no clear precedent. The university idea was struck, virtually *de novo,* by scholars and aristocrats of the enlightenment from only a few fleeting practical examples and with only a passing glance at history. It was an idea deriving force as much from reaction to intellectual chaos as from consolidation of intellectual growth.

At the end of the eighteenth century most universities in German-speaking Europe could be characterized as sites of rote disputation inhabited largely by pedants. Many genuine intellectuals regarded them with disdain. This situation had existed for at least a century, if one judges from instances such as the behavior of Leibniz, who essentially wrote the universities off in the seventeenth century and prevailed upon the elector of Brandenburg to found, instead of a university, an academy of science. Leibniz referred to universities as monk-like institutions concerning themselves with sterile fancies. Leibniz's academy, the *Societät der Wissenschaften,* was founded in 1700 in Berlin, but fared little better than the universities after Leibniz died in 1716. King Frederick William I (1713-40) treated its members contemptuously, even appointing three of his court fools presidents of the academy. The academy was later rehabilitated under Frederick the Great (1740-86) as the Prussian Academy of Arts and Sciences (*Preussische Akademie der Wissenschaften*).[1]

During the eighteenth century, universities were increasingly described as "medieval," a term that had a clear pejorative connotation. A phrase often used at the time described the universities as "atrophied in a trade-guild mentality."[2] It was widely believed within universities that knowledge was fixed within closed systems and the only task of the university was to transmit what was known to students, usually by reading aloud from old texts.

This anti-intellectual characterization is, of course, unfair to some scholars and some universities especially as the criticism no doubt stemmed from a changing view of what actually was to be considered legitimate scholarship. A careful and convincing description and analysis of eighteenth-century German scholarly life has been provided by R. S. Turner who persuasively draws a balance of the academic issues in the university controversy as they were probably viewed by the participants themselves.[3] Nonetheless, a sign of the fragility of these rigid institutions in the face of enlightenment reforms at the end of the eighteenth century is the fact that in the reform period between 1792 and 1818 more than half of the universities in German-speaking Europe ceased to exist.[4] There were, however, three universities that for varying brief periods in the eighteenth century provided a glimpse of what an intellectually exciting university could be. Two of these, Göttingen and Halle, were founded explicit as "reform" institutions, and the third, Jena, benefited by its proximity to the intellectual center of the German enlightenment.

Göttingen was founded in 1737 near the border with Prussia in the electorate of Hanover, whose elector at the time happened also to be King George II of England, and the university remained under the influence of the British Crown throughout the century. Cultivating an air of aristocratic restraint, Göttingen nurtured the more modern disciplines, particularly mathematics and the sciences, and stressed law, history, and politics to attract the sons of nobility. Halle, a Prussian university, was founded in 1694, partly in reaction to the sterile curriculum at Leipzig. Instrumental in its establishment were two precursors of the enlightenment, C. Thomasius and A. H. Francke. Thomasius made it the first university in Germany at which lectures were held in vernacular German rather than Latin. During the early part of the eighteenth century the philosopher Christian Wolff helped to make Halle the leading "modern" university in Germany.[5] Jena was founded in 1558 as a result of theological differences with Wittenberg rather than from any impetus for reform. In the eighteenth century it was located in the small duchy of Saxe-Weimar, but it was within the Prussian sphere of influence and was often regarded as a university serving Prussia. Goethe, during his years as a poet in Weimar, was also by invitation a minister in the government of the duchy and occasionally arranged university appointments at Jena. Thus, Schiller lectured at Jena in history in 1789. The school of philosophy known as German idealism flowered there in the late eighteenth and early nineteenth centuries, a time when Fichte, Schelling, and Hegel all held professorships at Jena.[6]

At the beginning of the nineteenth century, nevertheless, the reputation of universities generally was so poor in Prussia that J. von Massow, the minister of justice who was responsible for higher education, advocated that the university as an institution should be totally eliminated and replaced by unrelated professional academies serving special needs.[7] At the same time the city of Berlin, which had grown and become cosmopolitan following the end of the Seven Years' War in 1763, became a new focus of intellectual activity.[8] Fichte, for example, after being forced to leave Jena in 1799 on suspicion of atheism, spent some time at the University of Erlangen, but then began to drift away from university life altogether. Independent of any university he began to hold increasingly more frequent and highly successful "private" lectures in Berlin, including his widely heard and influential "Addresses to the German Nation" in 1807-8. Such lectures by Fichte, and occasionally by others, were widely attended by the elite of Berlin society, including many ministers of King Frederick William III. One minister who listened and was impressed was K. F. Beyme, who was later to become the king's confidant, and for a short time, principal minister. Beyme began to concern himself with how the intellectual resource represented by these private lectures could best be organized for the Prussian state, and as early as 1803 began soliciting essays from prominent scholars on the possibility of a new institution of higher education.[9]

There was clearly a high level of intellectual activity in Prussia at the beginning of the nineteenth century, but it was disorganized and dispersed and there were widespread doubts it could survive within existing institutions. The critical event which forced a resolution of this problem, thus leading ultimately to the creation of a new university in Berlin, is generally acknowledged to be the humiliating defeat of the Prussian army by Napoleon at the battlefield outside Jena on 14 October 1806. Napoleon closed the universities in Jena and in Halle. In August of 1807 a delegation of the former faculty from Halle, led by professor of law H. Schmalz, a university functionary, sought an audience with Frederick William at Memel in East Prussia to request that their university be reopened in Berlin. The king is said to have replied, with a mixture of sarcasm and resignation, "That's nice! The state must replace with intellectual strength what it has lost in material resources."[10]*

It was at this time that Beyme was the king's most influential minister, and he immediately solicited suggestions on a new institution of higher learning from Fichte as well as from others. He had obtained a document on this topic earlier from the classical philologist F. A. Wolf. The theologian-philosopher F. E. D. Schleiermacher carefully prepared and submitted another. These developments began to crystallize a year later when, in the fall of 1808, an unsuspecting Wilhelm von Humboldt returned home to Berlin from his post as envoy to the Vatican on what he expected to be a brief vacation visit.

*The remark of the king is apocryphal, and it may be falsely attributed to him. It has nonetheless been widely repeated in accounts of the incident and clearly appears to capture the sentiment of the court. The only first-hand report attributing the remark to the king comes from Schmalz himself, whose romanticized accounts of the incident have sometimes been questioned.

THREE
WILHELM VON HUMBOLDT AND THE IDEA
OF THE UNIVERSITY: BERLIN, 1809-1810

The figure of Wilhelm von Humboldt has come to assume extraordinary importance in perceptions of the founding of the new German university in Berlin. He is often referred to simply as "Father of the University," where the latter term is meant in the definitive and universal sense.[1] The concept of the German university in its most influential and best understood form is conveniently described as the "Humboldtian" university. A noted German scholar, the philosopher Hermann Lübbe, recently commented

> At the installation of new rectors, commencement ceremonies, that is, by preference at academic convocations, it is customary to invoke Humboldt's name at our universities. To be able to call on him is to legitimize oneself, and that is not only important for conservatives. Whoever, as well, intends to engage in reform makes his work with us easier by the proof that he really only hopes to bring about what Humboldt actually wanted.[2]

A striking example of the universality of Humboldt's appeal as a symbol of the rescue and re-creation of the university through a triumph of the German intellect is the continuing praise paid him by official propaganda organs of the German Democratic Republic. The original University of Berlin, whose buildings on *Unter den Linden* currently lie in East Berlin, was renamed the "Humboldt University of Berlin" by German communists in 1949 after the Free University of Berlin had been established in the western sector of the city.[3]

The tribute lavished on Humboldt is so extravagantly adulatory that the contemporary observer is led to believe that he not only devoted his life to the university but also created the institution alone from whole cloth. In fact, his commitment to the university and concern for it was limited to a brief sixteen-month period in the Prussian ministry, and there is little to suggest that he did much more than synthesize and bring to fruition, through competent management within the government bureaucracy, an idea developed in large measure by others. Whereas, for example, a substantial number of carefully developed essays on the idea of a new university had been prepared by scholars, philosophers, and bureaucrats at the time of the founding of the University of Berlin, there exists only one organized statement on this subject written by Humboldt himself.[4] This statement is but a brief fragment of an internal ministry memorandum that was not published until 1896 in a Humboldt biography.[5]

A further indication that Humboldt's enthusiasm at the opportunity to control the creation of the new university was at best restrained is the fact that he very much preferred to return to Rome rather than to accept appointment in Berlin. He was offered appointment as privy councilor in charge of the newly created section for culture and public instruction, within the interior ministry, where he would be responsible for all educational matters. He tried to turn down the impending appointment in a letter dated 17 January 1809, but the king remained firm. He finally relented when friends pressed him with the danger that a mere bureaucrat, like Beyme, might be appointed at so critical a time.[6] He was officially appointed as privy councilor and section director on 20 February 1809. He was relieved of duties in the ministry at his own request on 14 June 1810, five months before the University of Berlin first opened for instruction without fanfare on 15 October 1810. During his little more than a year in the ministry, he restructured Prussian secondary education and established the University of Berlin.

Prussia's defeat at the hands of the French was so total that the appointment of King Frederick William III's principal ministers was subject to Napoleon's personal approval. The most prominent candidates for chief minister were two experienced government reformers, K. A. von Hardenberg, who was serving as Foreign Minister, and Baron H. F. K. vom und zum Stein, who had earlier served as Minister of Finance. Napoleon distrusted Hardenberg, who was forced to retire in July of 1807, and recommended that the king appoint Stein, of whose anti-Napoleonic sentiments he was unaware. Stein was confirmed as chief minister, assuming wide powers, on 4 October 1807, and the influential Beyme was immediately transferred to a peripheral ministry of little importance. It was Baron Stein who recommended to the king that Humboldt be placed in charge of educational matters in the Prussian ministry.

In late 1808 Napoleon's agents intercepted a letter from Stein to the Hessian court encouraging revolt against Napoleon, and this led to Stein's dismissal from the ministry on 24 November 1808. Napoleon subsequently declared him a public enemy and six weeks before Humboldt assumed office Stein fled into hiding in Bohemia, on

5 January 1809. Thus, the chief minister during Humboldt's tenure was neither Stein nor Hardenberg, but K. vom Stein zum Altenstein, whose leadership is generally regarded as weak and ineffectual. With Napoleon's approval, Hardenberg was finally called from retirement to assume the position of chief minister on 6 June 1810, the same week that Humboldt left the ministry. It is, therefore, erroneous to regard the founding of the University of Berlin as an integral part of the Stein-Hardenberg era of reform in Prussia; Humboldt held a unique position of authority during the period of the founding.

Humboldt did not agree with Hardenberg on many matters, and one reason he cited for his resignation was his disappointment that the section on culture and public instruction was not elevated to the status of an independent ministry, a position Hardenberg was known to have little sympathy for. The date of 14 June 1810 thus marks the end of Humboldt's formal involvement with the educational affairs of Prussia. He was, however, called back to governmental service as a privy councilor in other matters, even to the extent of representing Prussia at the Congress of Vienna in 1815 (he is depicted among the diplomats assembled in the painting by Jean Baptiste Isabey of the Congress of Vienna). As the force of reaction became all too clear, Humboldt retired fully from public affairs in December of 1819. He devoted the rest of his life to scholarly pursuits and died at his home in Berlin on 8 April 1835.[7]

It is worth trying to resolve the seeming paradox of how Humboldt, whose commitment of both time and effort was not nearly as great as others, could nonetheless be so universally credited with the concept of a new university. The resolution lies in the intersection of two historical circumstances. First, Humboldt was a clear-thinking intellectual with practical government expertise who could in fact firmly insure that the University of Berlin be established auspiciously and with the highest intellectual standards. Second, the *Zeitgeist* provided the possibility for an individual person, one could say a hero, to unify and resolve authoritatively the tension generated by various passionately held ideas of similar intent but very different detail. The University of Berlin was founded at a time when the enlightenment and *Sturm und Drang* were converging on idealism and romanticism. It was an age of heroes, of Napoleon, Beethoven, Schiller, Goethe. It has been persuasively argued that, in America, the Constitution of the United States could not have been achieved had the convention not been chaired by George Washington. This is less because Washington contributed substantively to the debate than because he was a figure of unquestioned respect and authority who imposed a unity of purpose that compelled a successful outcome.[8] In Prussia, in the same age, a similar role was played by Wilhelm von Humboldt in the creation of a new university.

Humboldt's father was an officer in the Prussian army and, by virtue of family, Humboldt had easy access to the aristocracy of Prussia. Yet his credentials as a liberal, and as an intellectual caught up in the issues of his era, were impeccable. Along with his younger brother, the well-known explorer and geographer Alexander, he was educated by private tutors in his father's home. He studied briefly at the universities of Frankfurt (oder) and Göttingen. He was serving in a minor capacity in the Prussian court when at age twenty-two, in 1789, he published his essay "On Religion," which questioned religious dogmatism and defended freedom of intellectual inquiry. The essay was correctly regarded as a critical attack on the Prussian government's enforcement of a harsh dogmatist edict in 1788. Three years later he quit government service and published his most influential essay, "Ideas on an Attempt to Define the Limits of the Effectiveness of the State."[9] This piece is the unquestioned monument of German liberal thought; it provided the unified driving force for liberals in Germany throughout the nineteenth century, and inspired John Stuart Mill's essay "On Liberty." Humboldt was a close friend of both Schiller and Goethe, and spent the period between 1792 and 1801 partly in Jena and Weimar, later in Paris and in Spain, studying literature and publishing pieces of literary criticism. Goethe said of him that Humboldt was the only man in all of Germany with whom he freely wished to speak, and to whom he could freely talk.[10] In 1801 Humboldt again accepted government service, this time in Rome where he could be close to antiquity and develop his scholarly interests in anthropology, philology, and linguistics.[11]* He was deeply immersed in these pursuits when he returned to Berlin in the fall of 1808.

Upon assuming office in the ministry in Berlin in early 1809 Humboldt began to work with the idea of a new university, and sought assurances from a few leading scholars, such as Fichte and Schleiermacher, that they would accept professorial appointments. He was just as active at this time, however, in reorganizing and consolidating elementary and secondary education in Prussia.

---

*Humboldt was no dilettante in these matters. In a recent book which attempts to show what linguistic thinking from the past is applicable and relevant to modern linguistics, Chomsky focuses on Humboldt: "There is no single individual who can be shown, on textual grounds, to have held all the views that will be sketched; perhaps Humboldt, who stands directly in the crosscurrents of rationalist and romanticist thought and whose work is in many ways the culmination as well as the terminal point of these developments, comes closest to this."

At the elementary level, Humboldt brought both elementary schools* and teacher-training colleges under close state supervision and facilitated the introduction of the methods of the Swiss educational reformer, J. Heinrich Pestalozzi.[12] The first of what were to become many Pestalozzian seminaries in Prussia, which revitalized elementary education throughout the state, was established in Königsberg during Humboldt's tenure in the ministry. Pestalozzi's pioneering advocacy of effective elementary education for all social classes was well known to enlightenment intellectuals in Prussia. Much of Fichte's inspirational "Addresses to the German Nation" was devoted to an appeal for a spiritual regeneration of the people through the methods of Pestalozzi. The Prussian queen, Louisa, was particularly impressed with these ideas and it was she who personally arranged for seventeen leading figures in elementary education in Prussia to be sent in the Fall of 1808 to Pestalozzi's institute in Yverdon, Switzerland, for training directly under Pestalozzi. Thus, Humboldt was not directly responsible for introducing Pestalozzian methods into Prussia, although he supported such initiatives as had already been undertaken and sought to enhance their effectiveness. He had some reservations about the method itself, believing at first that it emphasized rote mechanical means of learning at the expense of

---

*The foundation for universal elementary education in Prussia had been laid early in the eighteenth century when King Frederick William I issued the first order requiring attendance at school in 1717. Frederick the Great prescribed detailed regulations including compulsory education between the ages of five and fourteen, in 1763. However, in 1809 elementary schools were still a novelty in many areas and differed significantly in quality. Although a teacher-training college had been established in Prussia as early as 1697, by Francke at Halle, teacher-training methods were still generally poor and disorganized.

imagination, but he ultimately became an advocate. The Pestalozzian seminary was established in Königsberg by K. A. Zeller, a renowned disciple of Pestalozzi, who accepted a renewed call to Prussia from Humboldt after refusing an earlier call. The seventeen returned in 1811, made contact with Zeller, and then proceeded to found Pestalozzian seminaries throughout Prussia.[13]

Unquestionably, however, Humboldt's most important educational reforms aside from the new university were at the secondary level, which he began with the Königsberg school plan and the Lithuanian school plan of 1809.[14] These established the *Gymnasium* as the cornerstone of secondary education. The idea of the *Gymnasium* was carefully formed in symbiotic relationship to the university; each institution was to enhance the prestige and ensure the survival of the other. That Humboldt sought a clear and intimate relation between the secondary school and the university is indicated in part by his assertion that "it is principally the responsibility of the state to organize its secondary schools so that they work hand in hand with [*gehörig in die Hände arbeiten*] the institutions of higher learning." He also reflected broadly on the intellectual interplay between the two levels of education:

> It is a further characteristic of institutions of higher learning that they always treat knowledge [*Wissenschaft*] as an as yet unsolved problem, and thus always stay at research, whereas the secondary school learns about and deals only with well established and derived principles. The relation between teacher and pupil thus becomes a thoroughly different one than it has previously been. The former is not there for the latter, rather both are there for the sake of knowledge. . . .[15]

There were two key elements to Humboldt's reforms. First, he introduced mandatory state certification by comprehensive examination of *Gymnasium* instructors, which assured that only persons who had studied at a university would be permitted to teach at these institutions. This resulted in the elimination of large numbers of poorly trained theology students from the teaching staff of *Gymnasien* and greatly increased the status and prestige of the position of *Gymnasium* instructor which then became a respected career ambition.[16] Second, he universalized and placed under state control the final examination upon completion of the curriculum of a *Gymnasium*, the *Abitur.* Further, he enhanced its importance by granting anyone who successfully completed this examination the unequivocal right to enter and study at any university in Prussia.

The concept of a unified privilege-granting graduation examination, variously referred to as *Abitur, Abiturienten-examen, Maturitätsprüfung,* or *Reifeprüfung,* was not new. Such an examination was proposed under Frederick the Great and approved by him in the last years of his reign, although for technical reasons the edict was not actually promulgated until 1788, somewhat more than a year after his death. However, the clergy, whose power greatly increased under Frederick the Great's successor, Frederick William II, opposed the examination which then failed to develop any significance. When Humboldt assumed office in the ministry, there existed a variety of standard nine-year secondary schools with similar curricula, such as the *Gymnasium, Lyceum, Pädagogium, Collegium, Lateinische Schule,* and *Akademie.* After the formal establishment of the universal *Abitur**, all of these schools adopted the common name of *Gymnasium.*[17]

The first of the reforms, licensing the instructors, had two important consequences for the university: it provided a continual supply of well-motivated students, and it helped make central the importance of the faculty of arts and sciences. The principal consequence of the second reform, the standardization of the *Abitur,* was on the *Gymnasium* itself: it made successful completion of the *Gymnasium* the gateway to prestige and privilege in Prussian society. These reforms set the pattern in secondary and higher education for most of central Europe through the nineteenth century, and to the present day.

Perhaps reflective of the heroic age of which he was a part Humboldt developed just one overriding principle in founding the new university of Berlin: to appoint the best intellects available, and to give them the freedom to carry on their research wherever it led. He summarized the state's responsibility to the new university in a single sentence, "The crux of the matter rests on the selection of the men to be placed in activity." He was thoroughly unconcerned with the details of the new university, hardly ever mentioning, for example, organizational structure or bylaws, because of his conviction that individual strength of

---

*Humboldt was not able to complete all of the arrangements for institution of a universal *Abitur* during his brief stay in office. After his resignation, others, notably Schleiermacher, completed the work. The edict establishing the *Abitur* was issued on 25 June 1812. Although passing the *Abitur* granted admission to the university, it was still possible for students who did not take the *Abitur* to apply directly to the university, where a different admissions test was administered. There was thus a second opportunity, independent of the *Gymnasium*-linked *Abitur,* to gain entrance to the university. As the reform of 1812 settled and solidified, the *Gymnasium* grew in importance and the *Abitur* came to be regarded as the most appropriate test of university aptitude. Finally, on 4 June 1834, the government of Prussia abolished separate university admissions tests, and passage of the *Abitur* became the only way to gain entrance to a university. This action completed the development of the symbiotic relationship of *Gymnasium* to university by tying the two institutions unconditionally to each other.

intellect was the only important factor: "If ultimately in institutions of higher learning the principle of seeking knowledge [*Wissenschaft*] as such is dominant, then it is not necessary to worry individually about anything else."[18]

On the basis of preliminary inquiries among scholars, Humboldt concluded that an outstanding faculty could be assembled within a relatively short span of time. Thus assured, he sent a proposal to the king for the founding of a university in Berlin on 24 July 1809. The better part of a year was then consumed by the negotiations with potential faculty, as well as arrangements to receive the king's gift of the splendid palace* of Frederick the Great's younger brother, Prince Henry, to house the university.[19] The movement toward a new university had developed to such a point by 1809-10 that it was clear to many intellectuals this new institution was to be historic, important, and conducive to good scholarship. Therefore, many professors who were approached, particularly those residing in Berlin or Halle, felt honored and readily accepted appointment. An exception was Humboldt's friend and colleague in philology, F. A. Wolf, who stunned

---

*The palace, which still houses the Humboldt University in East Berlin, lies in the center of the royal residence surrounded by the Prussian Academy, the state library and the opera house. Upon arriving in Berlin and seeing the palace for the first time, the newly-appointed theology professor de Wette wrote to a colleague, "What a magnificent building, surrounded by magnificent buildings! It must be a pleasure to teach [*zu lesen*] there." (Lenz, *Geschichte Universitat Berlin*, p. 291). Before the university opened, Humboldt directed the words *Universitati litterariae* be inscribed in gold on the palace wall above the entrance. It is said that he chose this plural form, rather than the standard *Universitati litterarum*, to emphasize that the new university was a union of the academy of arts and sciences, the university, and the various research and teaching institutes.

Humboldt by declining. Negotiations were then begun, which were lengthy, complex, exasperating, and ambiguous. Finally, Wolf, a self-confident egotist who was unimpressed with extant examples of "universities," accepted, contingent upon a variety of vague understandings with the ministry. In essence, these boiled down to but one: that he never be required to attend a faculty meeting.[20]

By the following spring, sufficient progress had been made for Humboldt to feel that no further delay was necessary, and he advised the king to order that the university be opened the following fall; the order was issued on 30 May 1810. Among the faculty of the University of Berlin at its opening were W. M. L. de Wette (theology), J. G. Fichte (philosophy), S. Hermbstädt (chemistry and technology), M. H. Klaproth (chemistry), P. Marheineke (theology), J. C. Reil (medicine), F. K. Savigny (law), F. E. D. Schleiermacher (theology-philosophy), and F. A. Wolf (classical philology). A great disappointment to Humboldt was his inability to entice Gauss away from his home in Göttingen.[21]

Although a liberal on record as a critic of the authoritarian state, Humboldt wedded the University of Berlin in close and unbreakable union to the State of Prussia. Because this union bequeathed to subsequent generations a German university totally and intricately enmeshed within a series of states, most of them readily describable as authoritarian, it is worthwhile to explore how Humboldt viewed the relation between university and state. The German educationalist and Humboldt-historian Eduard Spranger comments that it was a strange fate for Humboldt to create the university in the service of the state because his ideals suggested that the university could best be created without the state.[22] However, there is little evidence that Humboldt ever seriously questioned that the state had a natural responsibility to provide education for the people on all levels, including a sound university. Humboldt's position on this matter was essentially that of the leading intellects of classical Greece, such as Plato, for whom he had the highest regard.

In fact, Humboldt worked actively to eliminate the remaining vestiges of private status in the only existing scholarly institution still retaining some independence from the state, the Prussian Academy of Arts and Sciences. Members of the academy vigorously resisted capitulation to the state, but Humboldt believed that the research functions of the academy were a state responsibility, and that the academy had to be integrated into the new university. In the end he drew up legislation for the king, which was approved on 22 September 1809 over strong protests from the academy. This law simply placed all of the academy's functions under direct state control and made it subservient to the new university about to be founded.[23]

It would be easy to dismiss the problem of state and university by noting simply that Humboldt had no choice since the Prussian national law of 1794 declared explicitly that universities were organs of the state. However, to the present day there have never been any private universities in Germany and the presence of successful private universities elsewhere in the world, particularly in the United States, has often raised the question of their complete absense in Germany. The fact that Humboldt, who occupies a unique position in German history as the one person most likely to have successfully encouraged and made possible the concept of private universities in Germany, gave the notion no serious thought is of more than passing interest.

One should not be misled by the American model, which is unique in the world for the number and significance of its private universities. At the time of the American revolution and during the era of reform in Prussia the identity of the "private" university in the United States was by no means evident. There was much talk of public education and a national university, an idea strongly supported by George Washington, without consequence. Thomas Jefferson, whose life presents in so many details a fascinating New World counterpoint to that of W. von Humboldt, proposed a comprehensive system of public, state-controlled, education through the university level to the Virginia legislature in 1779. Although he often had the bill resubmitted, the legislature was not ready to pass it. Ultimately, beginning in 1814 when he was 71 years old, Jefferson succeeded in establishing the University of Virginia, which became the first great public university in the United States. Over a ten-year period he recruited the faculty and designed both the curriculum and the buildings. "Private" universities in the United States had their unique contemporary identity assured only in 1819 when John Marshall's supreme court ruled in a landmark decision that the state of New Hampshire could not change the name of Dartmouth College to Dartmouth University and bring it under state control as a state university. Dartmouth's case was argued by Daniel Webster, an alumnus, who, according to some reports, moved both himself and Chief Justice Marshall to tears in his summation.[24]

Although Humboldt believed that the university was a state responsibility, he did seek to protect the university from potential abuses of financial power by the state. He thus proposed that the university be provided with a large grant of land from the king, an endowment, over which it alone would dispose. This proposal was provisionally approved, but quietly set aside by Humboldt's successor in the ministry, F. Schuckmann, who agreed with the king that this precedent would make the university too independent of the state.[25] Humboldt's lack of sympathy for a private university stemmed most likely from his basic conception of the state as a natural part of society, a conception probably little different from that of most of his colleagues.

The reformist ideals which were prevalent in Prussia for the first two decades of the nineteenth century implied the development of a new, enlightened, state. The fundamental concept of the state itself, however, was considered fixed and given. It was the obligation of the state to the people, and the relation of the people to the state, that was important, rather than some completely new idea of government. The contemporary German sociologist Ralf Dahrendorf, among others, has argued persuasively that, at least until quite recently, the concepts of state and society have not been clearly distinguished in German thought.[26] There is little or no evidence that Humboldt felt such a distinction was worth making. It is more likely the case, as Lilge puts it, that Humboldt shared the conviction of Pestalozzi, "who said that the task of modern education was not to nationalize man, but rather to humanize the state."[27]

It was clearly Humboldt's belief that by providing the best in education the enlightened state ensured its own enlightened development. The state provided higher education in the finest traditions of independent inquiry, and the students educated in this manner provided the state with enlightened ministers. In the following extended passage on the goals of the university, Humboldt reveals how this idealistic conception is to support the state:

Everything depends upon holding to the principle of considering knowledge [*Wissenschaft*] as something not yet found, never completely to be discovered, and searching relentlessly for it as such. As soon as one ceases actually to seek knowledge or imagines that it does not have to be pulled from the depths of the intellect, but rather can be arranged in some exhaustive array through meticulous collection, then everything is irretrievably and forever lost. It is lost for knowledge, which disappears when this is continued for very long so that even language is left standing like an empty casing; and it is lost for the state. This is because knowledge alone, which comes from and can be planted in the depths of spirit, also transforms character; and for the state, just as for humanity, facts and discourse matter less than character and behavior.[28]

But, in Humboldt's view, if the university was to humanize the state, the state had a clear obligation to control the nature of the university so that it maintained its high purpose. In this regard he appears as a wise paternalist.

The naming of university professors must be held exclusively as the prerogative of the state. It is certainly not a good arrangement to permit the faculty more influence over this process than a sympathetic and reasonable ministry would permit as a matter of course. This follows since antagonism and irritation are healthy and necessary at the university, and the collision between professors that comes about through the very nature of their task can also arbitrarily twist their point of view. Furthermore, the nature of the university is too closely tied to the vital interests of the state.[29]

As the last passage suggests, Humboldt was well aware that many of the great intellectuals he was appointing as professors at the university had feet of clay. In a letter to his wife he once dropped the exasperated observation, "To direct a group of scholars is not much better than to have a troop of comedians under you." Later, as he was completing his duties in the ministry he wrote again to his wife,

> You have no idea with how much difficulty I have to struggle above all with the scholars—the unruliest and most difficult to pacify of all peoples. They besiege me with their eternally self-thwarting interests, their jealousy, their envy, their passion to govern, their one-sided opinions, in which each believes that his discipline alone has earned support and encouragement.[30]

One senses in this passage, perhaps more lucidly than Humboldt could have at the time, how difficult it was going to be to maintain wise and enlightened servants of the state in the university-supervisory position of minister of culture.

Humboldt's characterization of the faculty in the aggregate was confirmed during the inaugural year of the University of Berlin. By arrangement with the ministry's founding commission, the law professor H. Schmalz served provisionally as rector at the opening of the university, but it was agreed the professors would elect a regular rector at an appropriate time. This election took place on Wednesday, 17 July 1811, at 6:00 p.m. and all of the twenty-three full professors who were on the faculty and residing in Berlin at the time arrived for the balloting. After four ballots, the philosopher J. G. Fichte was elected over the professor of law, F. K. Savigny, by a vote of eleven to ten, with three professors having finally departed the room, one having been called back quickly at the last minute to avoid an anticipated tie vote. Schmalz was the only candidate for rector who publicly declared an interest in the position, but on two of the three preceding ballots, before being eliminated on the fourth, he received only one vote, which was probably his own. Fichte was installed on 19 October 1811, for what was intended as a two-year term, but he was forced to resign after only a few months over a squabble with the faculty on a matter of student discipline: whether it was proper for two students to settle a classroom quarrel by a duel or whether it should be settled by disciplinary action of the rector. Under Schleiermacher's leadership, the faculty of full professors asserted that the university was not to interfere in questions of honor between students. Fichte was opposed to dueling, and disciplined the students. His resignation was accepted by the king on 16 April 1812, who then directly appointed Savigny to serve as rector rather than risk another unpredictable faculty election. Savigny spent much of his rectoral term in Prague on other business, during which Schmalz once more served as provisional rector.[31]

The evidence for strong differences of opinion among the first faculty, who had much at stake in the new university, underscores the common contention that Humboldt alone was responsible for the successful founding of the University of Berlin.[32]* This success was due in no small measure to the simplicity and elegance of the basic principles which Humboldt established as the cornerstone

---

*"It is clear to anyone who knows the founding of the University of Berlin that only the highly civilized [kulturstaatliche] neutrality of Humboldt as the state's minister, and the power he exercised through the issuance of law, brought about the reform. The reform certainly would have gone to ruin in argumentative fights between Fichte, Schleiermacher, F. A. Wolf and others had it been dependent upon the 'autonomy' of the scholars." Schelsky, *Einsamkeit und Freiheit*, p. 263. An example of the kind of strong views that were held at the

of the university and which, in the end, gave it its fame and influence in the world. In retrospect it appears possible to summarize these as three. During the nineteenth century these three principles became paramount in virtually all established and new universities in German-speaking Europe.

The first principle was the unity of research and teaching (*die Einheit von Forschung und Lehre*), which clearly established the importance of the scholar to the university. Simultaneously, it confirmed the value of scholarly methods of inquiry at the frontiers of knowledge. Humboldt acknowledged this principle by appointing the best scholars available, encouraging them to continue their research, and making them collectively responsible for academic standards and the award of degrees.

The second principle was the protection of academic freedom; *Lernfreiheit*: the freedom to learn, which gave students the right to pursue any curriculum, and *Lehrfreiheit*: the freedom to teach, which gave scholars the right of free inquiry. It was the concept of *Lernfreiheit* that hastened the development of the free-elective system in the United States and elsewhere. The concepts of *Lernfreiheit* and *Lehrfreiheit* were not new with Humboldt but had been developed within the tradition of universities over hundreds of years. These concepts were recorded most clearly for the first time, and advanced significantly,

---

time was Fichte's assertion that a university should be founded by first appointing a renowned philosopher as rector, with absolute authority. This philosopher would train disciples to teach at the university and his successor would be chosen from among them, thereby maintaining intellectual unity over time. A philosopher was always to be involved in the supervision, teaching and appointment of new professors of all non-philosophical disciplines. In Fichte's university, each full professor was to wear a special identifying uniform.

at the time of the founding of the University of Halle. King Frederick I, first king of Prussia, who had founded the university in 1694, visited Halle in 1711 for an academic convocation on his birthday, 11 July, and the rector, Nicholas Gundling, took this opportunity to deliver a forceful and evidently courageous speech on the value and importance of the royal protection of *Lernfreiheit* and *Lehrfreiheit*.[33] Humboldt's contribution was to make clear from the point of view of the interest of the state that this protection was central and essential to the survival of the university. Therefore, when Prussia finally got a constitution, in 1850, it contained in Article 20 the famous clause, *Die Wissenschaft und ihre Lehre ist frei,* which has been passed on to successive governments. The *Grundgesetz* of the Federal Republic states (Art. 5, Sec. 3) that "Art and science, research and teaching are free." [*Kunst und Wissenschaft, Forschung und Lehre sind frei.*] Of course, it continues to be true that the struggle for academic freedom is never won, but an ongoing process.

The third principle was the central importance of the Arts and Sciences (*die philosophische Fakultät*), which revitalized the liberal arts and gave the concept of pure research the significance it is now accorded. The concept of liberal education can be traced back at least to Plato. By the time of the late roman empire, the concept had been standardized to the seven liberal arts: the *Trivium* (grammar, rhetoric, and logic) and the *Quadrivium* (arithmetic, music, geometry, and astronomy). These seven liberal arts, or "arts and sciences," formed the basic curriculum of the medieval monastic school, and when universities began to form in Europe between 1200 and 1400 the largest faculty was understandably in the arts and sciences. All students had to start their studies with arts and sciences, and only after mastery had been achieved (the student having become a "master of arts") was further study in specialized subjects such as theology, law, or medicine permitted. This historical development had led to a situation in universities in the eighteenth century where the faculty of arts and sciences was considered the "lower" faculty, and the faculties in the professional areas were considered "higher" faculties. Humboldt not only abolished this distinction, but in appointing a philosophically sophisticated research faculty, he virtually reversed it. Lübbe, for example, describes Humboldt's contribution by stating that "The most important moment of university reform at the beginning of the nineteenth century is finally . . . the complete emancipation of the Arts and Sciences from the institutional domination of the higher faculties, particularly Theology and Law."[34]

Humboldt also made lesser contributions of importance. Among these were the consolidation of an organic relationship between the secondary schools and the university and, ultimately, retention of the name "university" itself. Universities in general were in such disrepute among intellectuals at the beginning of the nineteenth century that the Prussian scholars and reformers who sought a new institution in Berlin actively avoided using the word "university" in their essays and arguments. Humboldt's own memorandum from this era refers to "the higher scientific establishments of Berlin" by which he clearly means that one institution which he later called the University of Berlin. In the end, it was probably the transient successes at Göttingen, Halle, and Jena that made adoption of the name university possible. The title of university put this brilliant new institution in a historical continuum, thereby placing it in a strategic position to infuse its sister institutions of similar name in Germany and around the world with vital strength. A strong argument can be made, for example, that the development of universities in the United States would have been dramatically, perhaps drastically, different if Humboldt had named the new institution in Berlin an academy, seminary, or institute. The seemingly simple act of calling the new institution the University of Berlin may have been one of history's close calls.

FOUR
FRIEDRICH SCHLEIERMACHER AND
THE IDEA OF THE UNIVERSITY:
BERLIN, 1810-1817

On 3 June 1810, shortly before leaving the ministry, Humboldt established a four-person commission to draft provisional statutes for the university. He was himself a member, and continued to participate when he could, even after he left the ministry. The others were two ministry civil servants, also friends and colleagues of Humboldt's, W. Uhden and J. H. Süvern, and the philosopher-theologian F. E. D. Schleiermacher. Süvern wrote a set of notes preparatory to a rough draft, which he circulated to the other members on 20 June. Comments were also solicited from the highly regarded law professor F. K. Savigny. Finally, on 25 July, the notes and all comments were given to Schleiermacher, who was asked to prepare a complete draft for presentation to the commission. This romantic conservative then structured the draft statutes largely along lines he had developed in the essay on universities he had written earlier, in 1808-9, entitled "Opportune thoughts on universities in the German sense."[1] Rather than propose some radical new organization, as Fichte advocated, Schleiermacher sharpened and strengthened traditional notions of university structure. The result was the *Ordinarienuniversität*, the university of full professors, an affirmation in a romantic era of a heroic model.

First, Schleiermacher retained the traditional four faculties that had developed during the middle ages: theology, law, medicine, and philosophy (*i.e.*, arts and sciences); but these were nowhere ordered by rank in the statutes from highest to lowest as had become common practice for German universities. Second, he retained the traditional composition of teaching staff in three ranks: full professor (*Ordinarius*, or *ordentlicher Professor*), associate professor (*Extraordinarius*, or *ausserordentlicher Professor*), and assistant professor (*Privatdozent*).[2]* But there were to be no hierarchical titles or distinctions within ranks, thus putting a stop to a developing trend for some full professors to be more formally honored and worthy than their colleagues.

Only full professors were considered members of the faculties of the university. The university itself was to be organized within faculties as a collection of institutes or seminars, each built on a single full professor with complete authority for his institute. Each full professor was individually to negotiate directly with the appropriate state ministry, rather than through the university, for the financial and material support of his institute. For aca-

---

*The translation of the terms *Ordinarius, Extraordinarius* and *Privatdozent* as full, associate and assistant professor cannot be considered precise, but is rather a convenience of style. The meaning of various professorial ranks and titles in both the U.S. and Germany has varied over the past 200 years, but there are now commonly three professorial ranks in the U.S., hierarchically ordered by professional status, and there were until quite recently commonly three in Germany, similarly ordered. It is on this basis that the U.S. titles of full, associate and assistant professor are used as approximate translations of the German ranks.

demic decisions, such as the award of degrees, there was to be a senate composed of full professors and elected only by full professors. To represent the university there was to be a rector, a full professor explicitly regarded as first among equals, *primus inter pares,* elected by absolute majority of the full professors to a two-year nonrenewable term.

Schleiermacher's draft was submitted on 24 August. During the next few weeks, the commission went over the draft line by line but made few substantive changes, finally approving the amended draft on 22 September. On 2 October 1810, the king approved the commission's final report establishing provisional statutes for the University of Berlin, officially naming the professors, and provisionally appointing deans of each of the four faculties, and a rector. On Wednesday, 10 October, the provisional rector, Professor Schmalz, called the first senate meeting of all full professors; 16 of the 24 full professors who had been appointed for the first term were already in Berlin and attended this meeting at which it was proudly announced that 61 students had already registered, including a prince, an earl, and 10 nobles. Actually, when the first semester finally got underway, the total number of students registered was 256. There were 117 in medicine, 57 in arts and sciences, 53 in law, and 29 in theology.[3]

Lectures for the first term began the following Monday. The total teaching staff in all professorial ranks giving instruction during the first semester amounted to 55 persons. Of these, there were 24 full professors, 3 in theology, 3 in law, 6 in medicine, and 12 in arts and sciences. The disciplines represented among the arts and sciences professors were astronomy, biology, botany, chemistry, classics, geology, history, mathematics, philology, philosophy, physics, and political science.[4] A festive inaugural celebration had been planned, but the matter of provisional statutes and attention to other details had prevented adequate preparation, so the ceremony was postponed, as it turned out, permanently.

Humboldt's successor in the ministry, F. Schuckmann, declared that the ministry would not accept the provisional statutes as the regular statutes of the university, arguing that issuance of permanent statutes was solely a ministry responsibility. However, he assigned Uhden the task of preparing the ministry's draft and Uhden made only minor changes in Schleiermacher's original set of statutes. In 1812, the ministry asked a commission of four professors, Böckh, Rudolphi, Savigny, and Schleiermacher, to advise it on the final draft. Schleiermacher was designated to write three of the nine sections: on the general definition of the university, on faculties and deans, and on the rector and senate; he used this opportunity to polish his ideas on university structure.

The only significant point of contention between the faculty and the ministry at the final stage of approval was that the faculty had grown accustomed to a senate composed of all full professors, and staunchly defended this view against the ministry's proposal for a representative senate of fifteen persons. The ministry's proposed structure was ultimately imposed upon the faculty, and prevailed at Berlin, and in similar form elsewhere, for more than a century. It consisted of the four newly-elected deans (one for each faculty), the four outgoing deans, the newly-elected rector, the outgoing rector (called prorector), and five full professors elected at large by all full professors. The ministry's administrative and financial representative, called in Berlin the *Syndikus,* elsewhere and later the *Kurator* or *Kanzler,* was invited to attend all meetings of the senate and could bring his secretary. The rector continued to be elected by an assembly consisting of all full professors; the first ballot was only for determining a list of three persons to be submitted for election on the next ballot; ties were broken by lot.

Following a long delay occasioned by the war of liberation against Napoleon and the Congress of Vienna, the draft statutes were approved by the senate of the University of Berlin on 11 March 1816, and the final permanent statutes were approved by the king and presented to the university a year later on 26 April 1817.[5] These statutes, although heavily influenced by one person, Schleiermacher, are infused with the ambition and self-confidence of a belief in romantic heroism generally shared by intellectuals of the era. With optimism characteristic of the age, the statutes also boldly assume that a wise state, emerging in growth from an enlightened society, will protect and nurture its intellectual resources in the university.

Although universities in other parts of Germany had no formal relationship with Prussian universities through the nineteenth century, the statutes of the prestigious University of Berlin exerted strong influence on the various administrative agreements by which universities in other areas, such as Baden, Württemberg, and even Bavaria, were governed. Thus, Schleiermacher's model university structure became the basic organizational pattern for all German universities up to the present time. This form of administrative organization, which remains basically unchanged even today in the Federal Republic, leaves a substantial controlling share of academic administration exclusively to the state through its Ministry of Culture.

FIVE
DEVELOPMENT AND GROWTH: THE
GERMAN UNIVERSITY IN THE NINETEENTH
CENTURY

Schleiermacher's strong advocacy of the university's right to nominate a slate of three candidates for each vacant professorship eventually prevailed over the ministry's claim for unilateral authority of appointment, but the ministry, although pledged to consider the slate, was still free as a matter of law to reject or ignore such nominations from the faculty. The convention by which each professor was to negotiate individually with the ministry for an administrative budget led to the development of two formal procedures which have been maintained to this day: *Berufungsverhandlungen*, "calling negotiations," and *Bleibeverhandlungen*, "staying negotiations." A candidate for a professorship enters *Berufungsverhandlungen* when he receives a call from the ministry responsible for a given university to assume a professorship. An established professor at a given university enters *Bleibeverhandlungen* with the ministry of his home university when he has received a call from a different university to assume a vacant professorship; he will thus also be engaged simultaneously in *Berufungsverhandlungen* with the ministry of the competing university. These negotiations are often tedious, may last a year or more, and cover the minutest detail. They are carried on wholly within the state ministry, *i.e.,* outside the university. It is entirely the ministry's responsibility to strike a bargain which will result in the appointment of a new professor, or the continued services of a valued established professor. Throughout the nineteenth and early twentieth centuries, these ministry-directed negotiations were effectively the only way a university could develop and grow in Germany.

The budgetary growth of individual institutes was determined principally by the number of students studying with a given professor. Since there was no prescribed curriculum for all students, individual students tended to study entirely within whichever institute they had chosen as a discipline of specialization. Since each institute was limited to one professor, and there was usually only one professor for a given discipline at any university, students who selected a discipline in effect chose to study with a particular professor and his advanced students. The level of advancement of a student corresponded roughly with the prevailing examination and degree structure.

The University of Berlin initially offered only one academic degree, the doctorate. Technically, the University of Berlin also initially offered in theology a "lesser" degree as well, the *Lizentiat.* This came about because of a long tradition of offering this degree in the field of theology, and Schleiermacher's belief that it was the appropriate terminal theological degree. Schleiermacher argued that the doctorate in theology should be reserved only for truly remarkable universal contributions. During the nineteenth century, the *Lizentiat* in theology achieved an equivalence to the doctorate in the other faculties and thus became the highest terminal degree in theology. In the Federal Republic the doctorate has now formally replaced the *Lizentiat* in theology. A curious and interesting historical sidelight is that the professors in the faculty of arts and sciences at the new University of Berlin were impressed by Schleiermacher's arguments for theology, and thus requested and received authority to award a *Lizentiat* in the area of arts and sciences. Their reasoning was that the arts and sciences in the weak universities of the day were generally so poor that their doctoral degrees were suspect. By awarding a lesser degree, and reserving the doctorate only for remarkable contributions, the faculty at Berlin hoped to rescue the prestige of the doctorate in arts and sciences. As it turned out, the faculty was of such stellar quality that its first doctorates quickly won renown, and there was never any need to resort to the *Lizentiat*, which in fact was never awarded by the faculty of arts and sciences.[1]

Although the doctorate was the only available academic degree at Berlin, the majority of students neither sought nor received this degree. For some, it was enough to study for a few years and then embark upon a career, often in the civil service. For most, the goal was to complete the *Staatsexamen*, which was the qualifying examination in a given discipline for teaching at a *Gymnasium*, or for entry into certain other civil service positions. Although this examination was the responsibility of the state, which administered it, rather than the university, the state contracted with university professors to construct and supervise the examinations. Therefore, students at the university were usually personally dependent upon their professors for instruction, advice, and guidance with respect to preparation for the *Staatsexamen*. Thus, although it was technically a civil service examination, the *Staatsexamen* strongly reflected university goals in higher education. For this reason, it came to assume the characteristics of a first degree at the university, which, in fact, it was not. There was no distinction of courses or subject matter for students who sought only to take the *Staatsexamen* and those who sought ultimately award of the doctor's degree; the curriculum was the same for both.

During the nineteenth century the tradition gradually developed of awarding a kind of academic degree, a "diploma" (*Diplom*), for academic achievement at the university roughly at the same level of performance as the *Staatsexamen*. This award was granted upon successful completion of a *Diplomprüfung* which was an academic examination that complemented, but did not duplicate, the *Staatsexamen* which was a civil service test. The difficulty in maintaining a distinction between these two examinations, which were often administered concurrently, finally led, in the twentieth century, to a general acceptance of the *Diplom* as the initial degree granted by the university. However, even today in the Federal Republic the doctorate is still considered the only universal academic degree, *i.e.*, there continue to be disciplines in which the *Diplom* is unavailable.[2]

A student who sought a formal academic degree, either for its own sake, for professional advancement, or from ambition to pursue a career as a scholar, secured permission from a given professor who agreed to supervise and direct the student's doctoral work. In the authoritarian climate of nineteenth-century Germany, this doctoral supervisor was formally called the student's *Doktorvater*, a term which quaintly persists today. Because it was a natural stage of study at the university, students usually completed a curriculum equivalent to preparation for a *Staatsexamen* before embarking on work towards a doctorate. Typically, a doctorate could be achieved about six years after the beginning of studies at a university. Many left the university after receiving the doctorate to pursue careers in the civil service or some area of professional life.

For those in possession of the doctorate who themselves wished to become professors it was necessary to remain in the university doing scholarly work under supervision of a professor until sufficient scholarship had been published for the university, through its senate of full professors, to judge the developing scholar qualified to give lectures to students in his own right. This process was called *Habilitation*, a qualifying inauguration. The concept of *Habilitation* developed at the University of Berlin as its outstanding faculty began overtly to concern itself with maintaining the prestige and high standing of the university through close attention to rigorous academic standards.

Although the concept of the qualification to teach at a university as separable from attainment of the doctorate had begun to develop at the beginning of the nineteenth century, it was still expected and standard practice for award of a doctorate to be sufficient qualification in itself. Schleiermacher strongly argued for this position in his university essay.[3] In selecting the inaugural faculty, Humboldt deliberately avoided this notion and aimed for a higher standard. The first commission on provisional statutes bowed to his judgment by stating that those doctors who wanted to devote themselves to teaching would be subject to a special test, to be devised, called the *pro facultate docendi*. The ministry later discarded this new idea and proposed to the four-professor advisory commission on permanent statutes simply that the doctorate be the sole qualification to teach at the university. The commission objected and stated that the faculty has the clear right to deny the privilege of teaching to anyone with a doctorate; however, no one could be permitted to teach who did not have the degree. The commission then developed the notion of *Habilitation* as the necessary prerequisite, this to focus upon a public lecture by the candidate on a theme chosen by the faculty or by the candidate.

Gradually a formal set of three requirements were developed to measure whether a scholar had qualified to teach at a university. These were critical acceptance by the faculty of a second major piece of scholarship independent of the dissertation (the *Habilitationschrift*), successful direction of a scholarly colloquium, followed by disputation, in which members of the faculty were the only participants, and finally, more as a ceremonial introduction than as a test, a public lecture. In 1838 the University of Berlin formally adopted the procedure of awarding the right of *venia legendi* in formal recognition to scholars who had met the requirements for *Habilitation*. The right of *venia legendi* thus became a kind of second academic degree.[4] By the end of the nineteenth century a *venia legendi* or some other formal certification of *Habilitation* was required for appointment to the teaching faculty of virtually every university in Germany. To attain a professorship, a "habilitated" scholar had to continue his scholarly efforts independently until called by some ministry to assume a vacant professorial chair. It was not uncommon for this waiting period to last twenty years or more, during which many impoverished scholars lost heart and left academic life, or died.

This brief sketch of the degree structure permits a description of the hierarchical structure of the teaching staff of a typical institute. Once achieving a doctorate an aspiring scholar could earn nominal wages from semester to semester by securing a position as assistant to the professor in the institute. Assistantship duties, which typically included such activities as reading the professor's lectures to classes of introductory and intermediate students and carrying out the professor's instructions with respect to his preliminary research, were then performed at the same time the postdoctoral scholar was attempting to develop a *Habilitation,* a process that usually took from six to ten years.

A scholar who had been certified as "habilitated" (*Habilitiert,* with the academic appelation now reading *Dr. habil.*) was permitted by the faculty to give lectures, privately but in his own name, at the university. The formal designation of such individuals was *Privatdozent.* The significance of the word "private" was that the instructor received no salary from the state and was, in fact, not a member of the faculty, but he was permitted to collect the fees paid by students attending his lectures. Dedicated scholars who sought academic careers derived modest incomes from their lectures and devoted the remainder of their time to the research which they hoped would ultimately lead to a call for a full professorship at a university. Occasionally, particularly in professional fields such as medicine or law, such scholars had independent careers of their own and lectured at the university as a sideline.

The notion of "private" lectures for which students voluntarily paid fees had been retained at least partly because of the distinguished tradition, including Fichte's addresses, that had developed in Berlin salons at the turn of the century. In practice, however, the "fees" for these "private" lectures were collected by the state as a service, and the state turned the collected fees over to the instructor. From the student's point of view, a simple tuition was paid at the Bursar's Office. From the instructor's point of view, the more students that could be attracted to a "private" lecture the higher the wages collected by the instructor. So-called "private" lectures were usually well-integrated course offerings of an institute and were often instrumental in preparing for examinations. Furthermore, there was nothing to prevent a full professor, who was also a salaried civil servant, from giving "private" lectures in addition to his obligation to provide "public" ones. By offering a variety of popular "private" lectures from time to time, many full professors became immensely wealthy; the ministry paid them their regular salary and also turned over the "fees" paid by the students in the "private" lectures. By the end of the nineteenth century the distinction between private and public lectures was thoroughly muddled, and this situation was accompanied by remarkable disparities in the incomes of various professors.[5]

When a *Privatdozent* showed continuing development as a scholar, but had limited prospects for a full professorship of his own because of the generally very small number of such positions, he was often offered the position of associate professor at an institute. This post, called *Extraordinarius* or *ausserordentlicher Professor*, was a tenured civil service position which paid a modest regular salary. An associate professor had some independence of action in curricular matters but was circumscribed by his necessarily deferential dependence on the institute's full professor; associate professors were not usually members of the faculty of the university, this being a right reserved exclusively to full professors. It was from the position of associate professor that there was the greatest likelihood of being called to assume a full professorship.

The concept of being "called" to a professorship was appropriate inasmuch as it was unthinkable for a scholar openly to express interest in a given professorship, much less apply for such a position. The customary procedure when a professorship became available at a university was for the faculty of full professors to establish a committee to search for the most prominent available scholar of distinction to join their ranks. Normally, the search committee wrote to all full professors in the given discipline at all German universities for suggestions to fill the vacant professorship. The frequency with which a given name was suggested then usually provided the means by which a list of three names, in rank order, was constructed. At the conclusion of the search, this rank-ordered list of three names was accepted or modified by the faculty, proposed to and approved by the senate, and supplied to the ministry, whose officials then undertook negotiations with candidates. An aspiring scholar could do no more than publish, maintain good relations with his mentors among the professorial ranks, and wait. As Paulsen dryly observed at the end of the nineteenth century,

> Of course, competition for positions occurs in Germany, but it is clearly not a public or recognized system; it is shameful to offer one's services. There is no shortage of persons who lean towards the view expressed by the cultural historian W. H. Riehl in his autobiography, "I never publicly applied for anything in my life, with the exception of my wife's hand."[6]

In summary, the teaching staff of a typical institute consisted usually of a hierarchical pyramid of several postdoctoral assistants, a number of assistant professors, some fully involved in institute affairs and others just occasional lecturers, a few associate professors (perhaps just one), and at the top a single full professor. It was, of course, a lengthy process before an aspiring scholar could hope to arrive at a full professorship of his own. By the end of the nineteenth century, the average age of an assistant professor in a German university was thirty-three years, of an associate professor was forty-six years, and of a full professor was fifty-four years; at the prestigious University of

Berlin the average full professor was sixty years old.[7] Developing scholars in an institute were heavily dependent upon the incumbent full professor, not only for such material matters as salary, office space, teaching load, and working conditions, which the full professor negotiated for them with the ministry, but also in intellectual matters. The limited number of full professors in Germany controlled the professional societies, the journals, and the review boards of the publishing houses. Thus an intellectual disagreement with a full professor could easily destroy the career of a developing scholar altogether.[*]

The pyramidal structure of the scholarly staff of a typical university institute, in which the bulk of the teaching and much of the research was carried out by sub-professorial scholars, quickly gave rise in the nineteenth century to a very important negatively-defined concept, the "non-full professors" (*Nichtordinarien*). At the founding of the University of Berlin there were many more full professors appointed to the teaching staff than associate professors, the assistant professors were on the whole part-time lecturers who otherwise held appointments at the Prussian Academy, and there were very few postdoctoral assistants. However, as the structure of the *Ordinarienuniversität* began to cohere, and the institutes began to grow and develop, the number of *Nichtordi-*

---

[*]Ringer, *Mandarins,* pp. 56-7, describes a case in 1916 where a full professor, Georg von Below, persuaded the faculty of the University of Freiburg to revoke the *venia legendi* of an assistant professor, Veit Valentin, essentially because Valentin wrote a critical review of a reactionary and polemical Pan-German treatise by Count Ernst von Reventlow. Below himself was a Pan-Germanist. The faculty defended its action, which made Valentin ineligible to teach at any German university, on grounds of the importance of maintaining friendly protector-protege relations between younger instructors and full professors.

narien on the teaching staff increased rapidly and disproportionately both at Berlin and elsewhere. Since these individuals were often highly prominent scholars in their own right, their complete disenfranchisement by the prevailing structure of academic government became a source of tension, often undiscussed, within the university. By mid-century the academic community was aware of a "movement of non-full professors" (*Nichtordinarienbewegung*), even though professional special interest groups, or "movements," were viewed with considerable disdain in aristocratic nineteenth-century Germany, and particularly by the academic community.

During the revolution of 1848, one of the most salient and articulate reform groups to emerge was the *Nichtordinarien*, who argued strongly for the granting of some kind of academic rights for the sub-professorial teaching staff at German universities; like virtually all ideas for reform during this period, these proposals were washed away during the subsequent reaction.[8] By the end of the nineteenth century, the tension finally erupted into formal organizations: in 1909, a union of associate professors was formed in Prussia (*Vereinigung ausserordentlicher Professoren Preussens*); in 1910, a union of German assistant professors followed (*Verband deutscher Privatdozenten*); and in 1912 the two organizations merged into a German union of non-full professors (*Kartell deutscher Nichtordinarien*).[9] The first formal demand of this group, which met with success, was to be able to participate in the election of rectors at German universities; although they won the right to vote, *Nichtordinarien* were not, of course, permitted to stand as candidates. Schleiermacher's romantic heroic model of all intellectual authority vested in a single mind, the full professor, did not anticipate the proliferation of so many dependent non-professorial scholars, and university statutes were consequently inadequate, in fact mute, on this issue. This unsatisfactory situation remained untreated until the mid 1970s. It continued to be a significant, perhaps overriding, source of tension in the German university.

The legal status of the university as a state institution administered from the Ministry of Culture presented genuine problems for the maintenance of academic freedom. In 1819, at the height of the European reaction to the French revolution, Metternich called the governments of several German states to Carlsbad, where a series of resolutions was adopted to control what was thought to be a subversive conspiracy at the universities. These resolutions included a pledge to maintain strict censorship of the press and of academic teaching, to establish a system of curators (*Regierungsbevollmächtiger*) at universities and schools that was charged with observing the spirit in which lectures were given, to suppress students' organizations, and to establish a central commission in Mainz to spy out revolutionary activities. These resolutions remained in force until the revolution of 1848.[10] A famous incident in German academic history is the dismissal and exile in 1837 of seven illustrious professors at the University of Göttingen, including the Grimm brothers and F. C. Dahlmann, because of their protest of the king's revocation of the constitution of the state of Hanover. There were also occasional dismissals in other German states of famous professors.[11]

At about the time of the establishment of Prussian hegemony over Germany in the Empire of 1871, the strength of German scholarship and the importance of the German university was becoming known in the rest of the world. The universities then became even more a matter of national prestige, and since the concepts of *Lehrfreiheit* and

Lernfreiheit played an important part in that role, dismissals of tenured professors became rare. However, the influence of the state on the university, especially in matters of opinion and policy, continued to be extraordinary. An enterprising reporter for the *Norddeutsche allgemeine Zeitung* published a carefully collated set of figures in the issue of 5 December 1901, which indicated that in the years between 1817 and 1900, the ministries of the various states had appointed significantly large numbers of professors to universities in disregard of the carefully proposed nominations forwarded by the faculty, indeed over the explicit objections of the faculty.[12] In the faculty of theology the numbers were 102 arbitrary appointments among a total of 311 positions for which the faculty had proposed nominations; in the faculty of law there were 86 arbitrary appointments among a total of 436; and in the faculty of medicine there were 134 arbitrary appointments among a total of 612. Unfortunately, figures were presented only for the three professional faculties and not for arts and sciences for which comparable data have not been compiled.

There were undoubtedly more subtle means by which the state exercised its "responsibility" with respect to the university. Since professors had to negotiate individually with ministry officials for increases in budget for staff, supplies, and support, a prudent professor would be cautious in expressing public opinion in areas likely to be of concern to the ministry. It hardly seems a coincidence that no supporter of the Social Democratic Party (SPD), which had been founded through a merger of two somewhat older parties in 1875, and no Jews not professing Christianity, were appointed to the professorial staff of any German university prior to 1918. At the close of the nineteenth century an assistant professor (*Privatdozent*) of physics at the University of Berlin, Leo Arons, made public speeches supportive of the ideals of the social democrats. The Ministry of Culture protested to the university and requested that the university examine his privilege to give lectures, specifically whether the *venia legendi* awarded Dr. Arons was appropriate in light of his public behavior. The faculty formally considered the matter, concluded that Dr. Arons's *venia legendi* was academically sound and that his actions as a citizen did not conflict with his function as assistant professor of physics. The state of Prussia then promulgated a law on 17 June 1898, promptly dubbed the *Lex Arons*, which for the first time made the state co-equal partner with the university in the granting of academic degrees. On the basis of this law the state then retroactively revoked Dr. Arons's *venia legendi,* thus depriving him of the privilege to teach at any German university.[13] Judging from such incidents it seems clear that almost a century since the founding of the new university in Berlin Humboldt's enlightenment vision of a wise Ministry of Culture acting on behalf of an enlightened state had not yet evolved.

Such incidents nevertheless tended to strengthen the resolve of the professoriate at German universities to articulate and defend the central concepts of *Lernfreiheit* and *Lehrfreiheit.* This German rhetoric of academic freedom at the close of the nineteenth century played a dominant role in the development and definition of this concept in the United States.[14]* At the same time, the not-

---

*The opening sentence of the initial "Report on Academic Freedom" published by the just-formed American Association of University Professors in 1915 reads, ". . . 'academic freedom' has traditionally had two applications—to the freedom of the teacher and to that of the student, to *Lehrfreiheit* and *Lernfreiheit.*" Of the thirteen signatories of the Report, eight had studied in Germany.

so-free authoritarian structure within the university, by concentrating virtually absolute power in intellectual matters in a few select full professors, helped to give the world the unique brilliance for which nineteenth-century German scholarship is known. The tension which characterizes the nineteenth century between liberalism and romanticism on the one hand and reaction and authoritarianism on the other neatly adapted itself to the enlightenment structure crafted by Humboldt and Schleiermacher, infusing and motivating it with intense intellectual energy. The heroic romantic ideal encouraged daring, startling, soaring subjective leaps of imagination while simultaneously the arrogance and security of the authoritarian culture permitted lengthy, painstaking, methodical, carefully-crafted monuments of empirical research and scholarship. There is scarcely a single academic discipline in the late twentieth century that cannot identify significant, in many cases crucial, contributions by one or more nineteenth-century German scholars. This fact is perhaps the proudest legacy of Humboldt's University of Berlin.

Another legacy of the mature German university of the middle to late nineteenth century is its overwhelming influence on the creation of the contemporary American university.* W. P. Metzger has estimated that more than

---

*It is worth noting that what U.S. scholars perceived as the German ideal was probably seriously distorted by the status of Americans as foreign visitors in Germany. Thus, for example, because their own careers were not dependent on the resident full professor, U.S. scholars tended not to be sensitive to the barrier a German full professor often posed to the careers of German scholars. Similarly, since visiting U.S. scholars usually knew exactly what they wanted to study and with whom, the problems of the young German scholar struggling with these fundamental questions went unrealized. As foreign visitors, U.S. scholars also had a direct access to full professors which very few native Germans enjoyed. See J. Ben-David, *Trends in American Higher Education*, pp. 90-1.

nine thousand Americans studied at German universities in the nineteenth century. Since there were no graduate institutions at home, and British universities severely restricted the number and kind of American visitors, most aspiring scholars in the United States simply had nowhere to go but Germany if they wished to do advanced study and scholarship in a discipline. After a few false starts were made at other institutions, the Johns Hopkins University opened as the first graduate school in the United States in 1876. Of 53 professors and lecturers who had been appointed to the staff of Hopkins by 1884, virtually all had studied at German universities, and 13 had been awarded a German doctorate. The Ph.D. degree itself was a German import. None was awarded before 1861 when Yale awarded doctoral degrees to three students for high attainments in its Department of Philosophy and the Arts. By 1876, when Johns Hopkins opened, the Yale precedent of awarding a "doctor of philosophy" degree was being followed in 25 American colleges. The "doctor of philosophy" had been assumed directly from the German *Dr. phil.* which was the principal academic degree awarded by the German *"philosophische Fakultät,"* or faculty of arts and sciences. In 1890, 164 Ph.D. degrees were awarded in the U.S., and that number more than doubled by 1900. In 1871, the total number of post-baccalaureate students studying in the U.S. was only 198, but by 1890 there were almost 3,000. Throughout this period of birth and development of the American university the dominant influence, the overriding ideal, was the model of Humboldt's enlightenment university.[15]

These chapters, 2-5, were written to provide a description of the nature and structure of the German university as it developed into its mature form in the nineteenth century, and to give some indication of its importance and influence. Without knowledge of this heritage it is not possible to comprehend clearly the significance of the processes affecting the German university today in the Federal Republic of Germany. The close of the nineteenth century is a convenient point of departure for the present because the mature German university of about 1910 remained virtually unchanged into the early years of the Federal Republic. As the historian David Schoenbaum has wryly commented, "By the end of the nineteenth century, the German university had become a very conservative institution—in fact, conservative enough to survive Bismarck, William II, and Hitler, attenuated but largely intact."[16] This is not to imply that there were not evolutionary changes during the Weimar Republic and the Third Reich, but rather that such changes as occurred were for the most part trivial or transient.[17] It remains basically Humboldt's University of Berlin that provides the context for understanding the process, the importance, and the drama of the intellectual and political revolution currently sweeping the contemporary German university toward a new and different future.

SIX
CONTINUITY: THE WEST GERMAN
UNIVERSITY AFTER 1945

The key to understanding the nature of the debate in the 1960s and 1970s about higher education in the Federal Republic of Germany lies in the perception of two relatively clear processes in recent history. The first is that the traditional German university, on the Humboldt model, was carefully and reliably reconstructed after 1945, much in the same form as Paulsen described it at the close of the nineteenth century.[1] The second is that this fascinating awe- and nostalgia-inspiring museum piece, a displaced living monument from a distant time, collapsed utterly toward the close of the 1960s. The collapse opened completely, and made vulnerable to real change, the issue of the nature, structure, and function of the German university for the first time in more than 150 years. Reverence for the university that is no more, and respect for the undisputed creative contribution it made to civilization, are important sources of the intensity and earnestness of feeling with which this issue is currently being pursued in the Federal Republic. The questions that have been and are now being formulated in the great public debate are not likely to be clearly resolved for many years to come, but the debate itself promises to be of historic significance for those who care about the concept of a university.

In 1945 the German university, like most German institutions, lay in physical and intellectual ruin. Many libraries and laboratories had been destroyed; of the twenty-three universities in Germany before the war, only nine remained relatively unharmed in 1945.[2] Although it was not clear that the majority of professors and students in the Third Reich had actively collaborated with the National Socialist dictatorship, it was at least known that instances of resistance were isolated, largely ineffectual, and did not command wide support. Therefore, to the extent that the allies sought to agree on a common educational policy for Germany the sentiment went beyond simple "denazification" to include thorough reform and modernization of the structure and function of all educational institutions, including the universities. The British and the Americans sought to delay the reopening of any universities for several years until a plan for reform of the universities had been developed. However, when the Russians reorganized and reopened the University of Berlin immediately in 1945, and the French reopened the undamaged University in Tübingen, with its personnel virtually intact, the British and Americans followed suit.

By the end of 1946 all of the universities in the area that now constitutes the Federal Republic had been reopened; the French had even added a new one in Mainz. As the allies found they were agreeing on fewer and fewer principles, efforts toward university reform continued separately in uncoordinated fashion. The Russians began to administer the universities directly in accordance with soviet political principles, and as important instruments of denazification. The British and Americans established joint commissions of scholars to review the situation and make recommendations. The most important result of this review effort in the west was the publication in the British and American zones in 1948 of the "Hamburg papers" (*Hamburger Gutachten*), also called the "blue brief" (*Blaues Gutachten*) because they were bound in a report with a light blue cover. Principally the work of German professors, some just returned from exile abroad, this report sought to fuse the Humboldt ideal to a model derived from contemporary British and American universities; even such notions as boards of trustees, and "private" universities, were entertained.[3]

However, further discussions of potential restructuring of the universities were essentially abandoned when the political situation suddenly changed significantly. A rapid succession of events cut the western zones of occupation off from the Russian zone and created a new state in Europe: a western six-power conference agreed on 7 June 1948 on plans for a "Federal Republic of Germany"; on 20 June, there was a thorough currency reform in the western zones which was followed by the retaliatory Berlin blockade; on 10 April 1949, the French zone merged into the already merged British and American zones; and on 23 May 1949, the *Grundgesetz* or "Basic Law," of the Federal Republic was proclaimed. In less than a year, political responsibility for the western zones of occupation in Germany had been returned to the Germans.

Although the *Grundgesetz* was initially conceived as provisional, it has since become, by circumstance, the Federal Republic's constitution. This 1949 "constitution" relieves the federal government of any responsibility for the universities, thereby placing universities under control of the laws of the individual states (*Länder*). In theory, each of the states could have developed different university structures. In fact, with minor variations, all of the universities followed a parallel pattern of reconstruction according to a well-remembered model. The contemporary German educational reformer Gerhard Hess suggests five reasons for failure of university reform to take root in Germany immediately after the war. These are, first, the preoccupation with the terribly difficult problems of just subsisting from day to day in a world that had been physically, economically and sociologically destroyed; second, the dependency for all important decisions on the approval of the occupying forces, which inhibited rather than stimulated creative efforts; third, the intoxication of students and professors of the war generation with the genuine intellectual contact that had been suppressed for so long which made consideration of structural change secondary; fourth, the emotional appeal for a general return to the time before the most recent horrible past, to the "good years" prior to 1933; and fifth, the loosening of the ties to a central state authority, which encouraged a reliance upon old and trusted traditions.[4]

The framework for rebuilding the universities was exhumed from the early nineteenth-century milieu in which the university was conceived and developed. In 1954, for example, the minister of culture for North Rhine Westphalia made the following remarks in defense of state administration of the university, which could just as easily have been made by one of Humboldt's colleagues in government in 1810:

> It is an error to believe that the budgeting and distribution of research funds, supplies, and professional staff positions, or the critical planning of space and priority needs, just to mention a few examples, could best be accomplished by academic agencies themselves. These sorts of

tasks on the whole place too great a strain on the sense of collegiality. . . . It is not because the state considers professors incapable of administration, or immature, that there are expressed misgivings about the notion of complete self-administration by the university in the economic and financial area, but rather because the work associated with it is simply not possible to accomplish, in the long run, along with a full teaching load and genuinely scholarly work.[5]

The following description of the contemporary German university was written for an American scholarly audience in 1966; it could just as easily have been written by an American scholar in 1890:

The chairman is often the only tenured and full professor in a department. He is appointed for life and functions as a one-man dissertation and licensing committee since the granting of the German university degree is congruent with certification. . . . the German Doctor of Philosophy remains an assistant to his professor for about 6 years. After this period, he writes another dissertation, the "Habilitationsschrift," for which the chairman's approval is again needed . . . he often has little choice in the initial subject selection and in the methodology of his work. The chairman's power reaches beyond the department, especially through his various editorial positions. This dual authoritarian role stifles many young researchers and undoubtedly hinders new avenues and approaches. Papers by the chairman or those which have his approval are usually published without further scrutiny, or style and length restrictions. This does not necessarily contribute to the clarity of writing. The authors' names are never omitted during selection procedures, but form an important selection criterion. The one-man decision cuts committee work and publication lag, but seems to invite bias and hinders criticism within many specialized areas.[6]

As recently as 1968 the average length of study required to receive a doctorate at a German university was somewhat more than seven years; to receive the *venia legendi* and qualify for an assistant professorship took an additional nine years; and to be appointed to an associate or full professorship required about seven more years. The average age of initial appointment as an associate professor in 1968 was about forty-four.[7] These figures are about the same as for the German university at the turn of the century. At the close of the decade of the 1960s considerably more than two-thirds of all "departments" (*Institute*) at German universities were still headed by a single *Ordinarius*.[8] It seems clear that Schleiermacher's romantic ideal of the *Ordinarienuniversität* was very much alive during the reconstruction of the German university following 1945.

SEVEN
THE GERMAN UNIVERSITY IN THE FEDERAL REPUBLIC: AN ELEGANT BUT POIGNANT ANACHRONISM, TO 1967-1969

The notion of professor as hero, a quaint anachronism carried over from Humboldt's conception of the enlightenment university, is not easily compatible with twentieth-century intellectual life. This conflict of a developed idea with an inappropriate circumstance is the source of much of the tension within the German university. At the time of the founding of the University of Berlin the appointment of a full professor as simultaneously head of an institute, with complete control over his discipline, typically involved the commitment of salary to the professor and perhaps one or two assistants, and a modest budget for the purchase of books and paper or, in the natural sciences, a few pieces of small apparatus for an office laboratory. Administrative demands on the professor were negligible, with the consequence that the extraordinary power endowed with a professorship was exercised principally in the intellectual rather than the material realm. The size and function of contemporary universities, however, and the complexity of more mature disciplines in the twentieth century, have very different implications for an institute director. Yet, some 20 years after 1945 the concept and structure of the German university was fundamentally the same as it had been 150 years earlier at its inception. An example of the kind of tragedy this mismatch of idea with circumstance can foster is provided by the fate of Professor Heinz Filthuth, director of the Institute for High Energy Physics, *Ordinarius* at Heidelberg.

Professor Filthuth is a well-known successful physicist. He was called to Heidelberg after several years with CERN's nuclear accelerator in Geneva. With much energy, and with the support of both state and federal government, he built a modern and productive physics department (*Institut*) at Heidelberg that specialized in the preparation of materials and the analysis of results from the accelerator in Geneva. He was the envy of his colleagues, particularly with his "administrative" talent; he was awarded more grants and had more personnel and apparatus than any other academic physicist. In March 1972, Professor Filthuth was arrested and placed in preventive detention while the government sought to recover 3.5 million DM in research funds unaccounted for. Ultimately 2 million was recovered, 230,000 was determined to have been used for private purposes, and the remainder spent for scientific purposes, but illegally and without normal bookkeeping procedures.

The Filthuth affair is dramatically illustrative of the consequences of condoning the anachronism of the early nineteenth-century *Ordinarienuniversität* in the midst of the twentieth century. The director of the German Research Foundation (*Deutsche Forschungsgemeinschaft*), Professor Heinz Maier-Leibnitz, took the Filthuth affair as the starting point for an essay on the difficulties the German professor has with administrative problems. For Maier-Leibnitz, a former *Ordinarius* at the technical university in Munich, where together with Rudolph Mössbauer he introduced the concept of a physics depart

ment in a modern sense and built the first German research reactor, the university administrative bureaucracy
is so awful that it is no surprise that Filthuth simply
ignored it and went his own way. Since the concept of
Schleiermacher's *Ordinarienuniversität* requires that a full
professor be simultaneously head of an institute, appointment to a contemporary full professorship may
often carry with it the nominal sole responsibility for an
annual budget of 1 million DM or more. Because the academic system tends to keep aspiring scholars in secondary,
very dependent, roles until appointment to a full professorship, the very first invoice a professor ever authorizes
for payment in his life usually comes immediately after
being appointed to a chair.

Of course, the state provides a civil-service apparatus
which it places at the service of the professor to help
manage the budget, but these administrative offices are,
in Maier-Leibnitz's words, "notoriously understaffed."
Furthermore, because the state administrators have no
professional academic capabilities, they can make no academic or substantive judgments, so they rely heavily on
books of arbitrary rules to protect themselves from im-
propriety. Professors often have unusual problems and
suggest creative solutions, but such suggestions fall on deaf
ears and everything has to be done by the book. Even such
relatively minor problems as arranging for compensation
for travel costs of visiting scholars require inordinate
amounts of a professor's time and energy; Maier-Leibnitz
maintains it took him five years to feel he could handle
the administrative affairs of his professorship, and that
was only because he had a good secretary.[1]

The frustrations and irritations of dealing with an
insensitive and unresponsive bureaucracy tend to result
either in resignation, or in limited warfare (*kleinkrieg*)

with the state administration. The result is that when a successful scientist like Professor Filthuth takes shortcuts around the state administration he can be assured of sympathy from his colleagues. However, contempt of the civil service and of the bureaucratic rules and regulations leads easily to abuses of the kind that brought Filthuth to ruin. On 13 November 1973, Professor Filthuth was sentenced to three years and six months in prison for perjury, fraud, and falsification of documents.

Although the structure of the German university appears under examination as a striking relic from an earlier era, it could be argued that it is just one conspicuous example from an entire society reconstructed along late nineteenth-century lines. Dahrendorf has soberly, but forcefully, made the case that post-war society in the Federal Republic resembles German pre-war society along many salient dimensions, and that the profound social processes that have accompanied modernization in Germany over the past one hundred years continue to unfold today.[2] This argument, which focuses on the confusion between state and society in Germany, and on the peculiar mixture of capitalism and social welfare that made early twentieth-century Germany resemble a contemporary version of a feudal state, can be enhanced by such observations as that, as recently as 1970, 70 percent of the gross national capital of the Federal Republic was owned by 1.7 percent of the families.[3] In the area of higher education it is clear that in the 1960s the university was the same very small preserve of societal elites as it had been in the nineteenth century.[4] In 1960, to take just a quantitative example, only 5 percent of all persons between the ages of 19 and 23 had achieved the *Abitur,* which permitted entry to university study.[5]

Whether or not one adheres to the view that the post-war period in the Federal Republic can be largely characterized by physical and social reconstruction, it is convenient to consider the recent past in two periods separated by the year 1969. The first significant shift in political power in the Federal Republic occurred in 1969, and it was accompanied by dramatic changes in domestic and foreign policy priorities. It is therefore possible to view 1969 as the end of an era.[6] That this shift took place tranquilly and within a framework of parliamentary democracy is not without significance; it is even possible to contend that the inauguration of an SPD* government in 1969 marks the first significant transfer of power by democratic constitutional means in any German state. To the extent such a contention is convincing it then becomes possible to assert that Germany first emerged in world history as a modern state in 1969. It is also convenient to view 1969 as a watershed year for the German university. Although no particular event in 1969 stands out clearly as symbolic of the close of an era for the university, there was widespread recognition, echoed in SPD party-policy declarations, that the traditional German university was no more, that a new university concept was to be developed.[7]

For the German university, the period prior to 1969 was principally one of reconstruction, accompanied by leisurely consideration of reform possibilities, followed

---

*The major political parties in the Federal Republic use initials as abbreviations in the following way: CDU (Christian Democratic Union); CSU (Christian Social Union); FDP (Free Democratic Party); and SPD (Social Democratic Party). The CSU is a Bavarian party that, in effect, represents the CDU in Bavaria; therefore, the CDU/CSU are for practical purposes considered regular partners.

towards the end of the period by a number of stunningly swift fundamental changes in structure and concept. Public discussion of the potential need for university reform was not abandoned after publication of the "blue brief" in 1948, but it proceeded slowly and cautiously. As David Schoenbaum puts it,

> The states were not about to surrender any of their prerogatives to the federal government, even for federal money. Professors, endowed by the Humboldt tradition with an authority even Louis XIV might have found a bit excessive, were not about to countervail their own power. Politicians, still sensitized by the Third Reich, hesitated to exert political pressure on the university. Schoolmasters, flesh of the old university's flesh, were not about to demand the curricular "relevance" that they feared would put them out of status if not out of business altogether.[8]

In 1952 the U.S. High Command sponsored and paid for a conference in Hinterzarten, in the Black Forest, on "Problems of the German University," which was influential in that it was cosponsored by the West German Conference of University Rectors, the Association of German Professors, the Ministries of Culture of each of the *Länder,* and the Federal Ministry of the Interior. Discussion at the conference was largely programmatic and resulted in no specific changes in the universities, but three issues emerged from the discussion, were gradually clearly articulated, and came to be recognized as serious problems.

The first issue was the need for financial assistance for needy students. The momentum from discussion of this problem carried the government and the universities into another conference at Bad Honnef in 1955, which resulted in a widely successful plan for personal subsidies from federal money for university students. The second issue was the recognition that the university structure, which created an untenable division of authority and responsibility between *Ordinarien* and *Nichtordinarien,* needed to be altered. Because this issue struck at the heart of each individual university no concrete changes were recommended but the fact that the issue was articulated and recognized as a problem placed it high on the agenda of potential reform. The third issue was the relationship between the university and the general public. There was widespread agreement that the university must make efforts to avoid being perceived as an exclusive preserve of the elite, as was the case in the nineteenth century, and to avoid withdrawing from public life into unconcerned isolation, as was the case during the Weimar period and to some extent during the Nazi years. American proposals for such agencies as boards of trustees and university public information offices were considered politely, but were regarded as so alien to European tradition as to be impractical. The concern for effective public relations was, however, genuine, and the commitment expressed at the conference by all parties to achieve this end was an important step in helping to bring the university into public consciousness in the late 1950s, thereby facilitating reform in the 1960s. The struggle with the concept of some kind of community agency to insure the public trust, along the lines of a board of trustees, led ultimately, five years later, to the creation of the federal *Wissenschaftsrat* (The Council of Science) which even today gently tries to guide federal efforts at reform.

The aim of the framers of the Federal Republic's constitution in divesting the federal government of responsibility for universities was to avoid powerful central control of intellectual life and thus to avoid abuses of the kind the Nazis sought to implement. However, the disadvantage of this model was that the eleven states (*Länder*) of the Federal Republic were cut off from access to federal funds for development of the universities. This became a major problem because university development is expensive and virtually all of the significant public financial resources of the Federal Republic were in the federal government, rather than in state governments. Creation of the *Wissenschaftsrat* was the first cooperative step between states and the federal government to try to solve this problem. This council was designed to be above partisan politics, to represent prominent nongovernmental interests for the purpose of insuring the public trust, and to contain sufficient governmental representatives to be informed of legislative and political constraints.

The council consists of two committees, each with twenty-two votes; a two-thirds majority is necessary for adoption of a proposal in either committee or in the full council. The academic or scientific committee consists of sixteen persons from academic life nominated jointly by the most distinguished scientific and intellectual organizations in the Federal Republic. These scholars and professors do not represent specific institutions but rather are individually considered experts on academic matters. The remaining six persons on the academic committee are prominent individuals from the private sector, usually industrialists, nominated jointly by the federal and state governments. All members are appointed to three-year terms by the president of the Federal Republic. The government or administrative committee consists of eleven representatives of state government, *i.e.*, one from each state, and eleven votes from representatives of various federal bodies and ministries. The council has no authority to make law, but may only propose recommendations, which must then be enacted by the individual state governments and/or the federal government. To the extent that agreement can be reached on common national policy it becomes possible to use federal funds for implementation of the proposals.[9]

The first reports and recommendations of the *Wissenschaftsrat* began to appear in 1960 and they were striking in their revelation of massive overcrowding in the universities, a portent of imminent crisis. The *Wissenschaftsrat* undertook the first sound systematic projections of current and future *Gymnasium* graduates (*Abiturienten*), and of university students, and these showed impending sharp increases on top of what was already an intolerably overburdened university plant. The first recommendations therefore focused on the need for rapid expansion, both of physical facilities and of teaching personnel. Owing to the favorable state of the economy of the Federal Republic in the early 1960s, the states and the federal government were able to provide the funds to finance this expansion, with the result that the recommendations were largely implemented: many established universities more than doubled in size, and a number of large new universities were founded and built.

Partly because of the perceived emergency in sheer numbers of students, and partly because of prudent political considerations, the recommendations of the *Wissenschaftsrat* tended to be forceful and bold when dealing with quantitative considerations such as the need for more spaces for students, but reserved and cautious—even timid—when dealing with such qualitative considerations as university function, organization, and structure. However, rapid quantitative expansion alone had significant consequences in weakening the structure holding together the traditional *Ordinarienuniversität*. To the

extent, for example, that large numbers of full professorships were created, the monopolistic control of a single
full professor in a discipline was necessarily severely restricted, and uncomfortably so, in that the unsettling
opinions of an unpredictable colleague now had to be
considered in matters of curriculum and the granting of
degrees. Because there were not enough qualified full
professors to meet the needs of the large numbers of students, the ranks of the *Nichtordinarien* swelled enor-
mously, both in number and in kind. Large numbers of
Gymnasium instructors, for example, or those previously
considered qualified to teach only at the *Gymnasium* level,
were recruited to teach lower-level university courses
(*Studienrat im Hochschuldienst*). The long-standing tension
between *Ordinarien* and *Nichtordinarien* over roles and
responsibilities in the university, unresolved in a history
of more than a hundred years, was thus intensified and
exacerbated. Finally, academic decisions of considerable
importance were being made indirectly by politicians,
economists, and engineers as choices were made to build
one kind of facility, a hospital for instance, rather than another, perhaps a library.

Although the *Wissenschaftsrat* entered the waters cautiously, it did begin gradually in the early 1960s to release
recommendations, in the form of "stimulative suggestions" (*Anregungen*), on the issue of qualitative university reform. With respect to faculty organization, it
was suggested that the "middle group" (*die mittlere Gruppe*
or *Mittelbau*) of the academic community be more pre-
cisely defined, and granted clear organizational and legal
rights; the middle group included essentially all *Nichtordinarien*, and was conceptualized as being in the middle between students on the one hand and full professors on the
other. It was further suggested that the traditional concept

of the faculty of arts and sciences, acting as a single corporation to represent the collection of otherwise autonomous full professors, be broken down into faculties of humanities, natural sciences, and social sciences, and within faculties into disciplinary groups like departments. With respect to curriculum, it was suggested that clear stages be developed with appropriate degree structures, between basic studies, applied or continuing studies, and advanced studies.[10]

Although the recommendations on university reform were published benignly as simple suggestions, they appeared just at the time when huge expenditures were being made for university physical plant and personnel throughout the Federal Republic. Because higher-education budgets had quickly become by far the largest part of any individual state budget, the minister of culture in each state became one of the most prominent, in some instances most powerful, political functionaries in each state. The public could not ignore developments on so grand a scale, and the recommendations of the *Wissenschaftsrat* thus became the focus of much debate on the general issue of university reform. Another element contributing to the prominence of national consideration of this issue in the 1960s was the fact that about half of the top editors in the mass media were themselves dropouts from overcrowded universities and had a sharp axe to grind.[11]

The breezes of liberal reform began to blow throughout all sectors of the higher education establishment. Perhaps the most important symbolic event of this optimistic period was the determination of K. G. Kiesinger, later chancellor of the Federal Republic, to help found a new reform university on the shores of Lake Constance in his native Baden-Württemberg. The University of Constance was established by the state legislature on 27 February 1964, and its founding board of distinguished academic scholars and reformers, guided principally by Waldemar Besson (political science), Ralf Dahrendorf (sociology and economics), and Gerhard Hess (romance languages), prepared an organizational structure based largely upon the recommendations of the *Wissenschaftsrat*.[12]

In a very short time, about five years since its founding, the *Wissenschaftsrat* had identified and made public a number of the most serious university problems, and initiated a process of change whose outcome is still uncertain. As the process accelerated, as hopeful optimism turned to anxiety, and as the purpose of reform was severely challenged by ideologies of the right and the left, the *Wissenschaftsrat* faded from the center of attention. Its stable presence, however, and its moderate voice, have provided an unseen anchor during a heavy storm that might otherwise have destroyed the German university altogether.

Unfortunately, the desperate material plight of the universities in the 1950s was so severe that, coupled with the increasing proportion of students proceeding to university study in the 1960s, even the extraordinary financial investment of the Federal Republic made hardly any impact at all on the quantitative problems it was designed to correct. Between 1950 and 1970 the proportion of 19-year-olds entering universities increased from 3.5 percent to 8.5 percent; the actual number of new students entering universities was about 25,000 in 1950 and 65,000 in 1970.[13] In 1968, the average ratio of students to "habilitated" professors, *i.e.*, those instructors formally recognized as qualified to teach at the university, was 58 to 1 in the arts and sciences. If one considers only *Ordinarien*, *i.e.*, just full professors, the average ratio was 87 to 1. The ratios were considerably worse in other commonly-studied fields such as law, 97 to 1, or business (*Wirtschaftswissenschaften*) 113 to 1.[14] To help shoulder the teaching burden, large numbers of predoctoral students were employed as university instructors. In 1966, two-thirds of all academic positions in German universities were held by such "assistants."[15] The persistence required of students to be able to complete their studies showed little sign of abating. Between the years of 1950 and 1965 the percentage of students enrolled in their ninth or higher consecutive semester at the university increased from 12.4 to 30.5, and in the eleventh or higher semester from 2.5 to 16.8.[16] These extraordinarily trying conditions for learning had a significant toll on students: dropout rates averaged about one-third of male students, and one-half of female students.[17] Such conditions led Schoenbaum to comment, accurately, "By the mid-60s the German university was a kind of disaster area: over-filled, underfinanced, its future apparently a half-century behind it."[18]

During this same period when material conditions appeared to be going from bad to worse in the universities, significant unsettling social and political uncertainties were building within the Federal Republic. Prior to 1963, the destiny of the Federal Republic was almost universally perceived as linked inextricably to the United States; this era culminated in a kind of national frenzy with President Kennedy's visit to Berlin. This was followed by rapid disillusionment with American ideals in the wake of the assassinations in the U.S., the growing American war in Indochina, the credibility gap, race riots in U.S. cities, and the events which led ultimately to the Kent State tragedy. Furthermore, the developing critical attitude toward the U.S., brought on by disillusionment, took place simultaneously with the reemergence of Germany as a force in international affairs, which caused a reexamination of the Federal Republic's policies with respect to eastern Europe. Finally, within the Federal Republic there was domestic uncertainty when Adenauer finally relinquished political control, under pressure, to an aging heir-apparent, Erhard, in 1963. The search for a more stable future led in 1966 to the "grand coalition" of CDU and SPD with Kiesinger as chancellor and Brandt as foreign minister. These developments in public life injected an element of political uncertainty, perhaps political possibility, into a German student culture already beginning to react to oppressively frustrating physical and intellectual barriers to learning.

Student unrest in the Federal Republic during the 1960s must be viewed as part of a larger international phenomenon in the west, in spite of national conditions uniquely conducive to it. The University of California at Berkeley experienced the long summer of discontent associated finally with the "free speech movement" in 1964, and this event clearly influenced the first student protests over the substance and role of student political advocacy at the Free University of Berlin in 1964-5. In May 1965, student discontent escalated in Berlin with a boycott of all lectures in political science; the protest began to assume a more narrow focus specifically against traditional structure and function in the university, and of advocacy of university reform. On 22 June 1966, 3,000 students at the Free University of Berlin staged the first sit-in in the Federal Republic, demanding that student viewpoints be considered on matters that affected students; a petition signed by 6,000 students was presented.

In January of 1967, the rector of the Free University, H. J. Lieber, reported to the annual meeting of the West German Conference of University Rectors that the events in Berlin should not be viewed as an isolated oddity, that student protest was certain to spread to the rest of the Federal Republic. His remarks were met with skepticism and did not dampen the cordial atmosphere characteristic of these meetings. The next meeting of the conference, in May of 1968, was somber, defensive, and anxious. Between the two meetings, the Shah of Iran had visited Berlin. On 2 June 1967, he was met at the opera by a large crowd of students protesting political persecution in Iran; the police charged the crowd and during the confrontation, a student, Benno Ohnesorg, was shot and killed by a policeman. Within weeks, active student protest had spread to virtually every university in the Federal Republic.[19]

Student protest, on top of the budget-consuming ambitious university building program, pushed the issue of university reform in the Federal Republic squarely into the middle of public life, thereby thoroughly politicizing it. On the whole, both politicians and the mass media finally lost patience with the failure of the universities, *i.e.*, the professoriate, to take any significant steps toward putting its own house in order. Public sentiment began strongly to reflect the view that if the universities would not reform themselves from within, the state and federal government would have to accomplish reform from above, and impose it. Because of the total dependence of the German university upon the state, this alternative was entirely feasible. However, the question of what kind of reform to accomplish remained an open question; upon close examination the issues of the function and structure of the university were complex and difficult to resolve. These two factors, the sense of an impending political solution to university reform, and the lack of any consensus on the nature of the solution, intensified the public political debate and began seriously to frighten and alienate the professoriate.

The earlier analysis by the *Wissenschaftsrat* of three natural groupings within the university: students; *Nichtordinarien* ("middle academics" or *Mittelbau*); and *Ordinarien* (full professors) crystallized gradually into advocacy, principally by students, of a "triple parity" model of power-sharing within the university.[20] This argument held that each university should have a governing agency, a senate, in which students would have 33 percent of the votes, middle academics would have 33 percent, and full professors would have 33 percent. "Triple parity" became a burning political issue and when the state of Lower Saxony incorporated the concept into a new university reform law, a group of law professors at Göttingen promptly filed suit against it in the federal constitutional court. The grounds for contest were simple: the professors argued that the famous constitutional provision by which "research and teaching are free" would be violated if full professors did not possess an absolute majority vote on academic matters.

The political debate was greatly exacerbated by a national government in the form of a grand coalition of the two major parties. Each party compromised somewhat the principles of the other and arrived at agreements which could in effect be dictatorially enforced because parliamentary opposition consisted only of the small token voice of the liberal FDP. Deprived of a governmentally sanctioned opposition voice, both students and professors turned more explicitly to radical positions reflecting their sense of alienation.[21]

The students consisted almost entirely of a generation raised after the war. Strong lessons on the virtues of democracy had been woven into the curricula of the primary and secondary schools these students attended under the watchful concern of the governments of the former allied occupation forces. Upon reaching adulthood, their first encounter with society was a nineteenth-century relic which resembled suspiciously the antidemocratic authoritarian institutions they had virtuously learned to distrust. Thus, their principal concern was for "democratization" of the university.

In the eyes of many students, the German university was not serving the needs of society but was instead simply generating apologists for an increasingly conservative culture in which the antidemocratic tendencies of the period from the turn of the century to 1945 were markedly reasserting themselves. Because most of these students had completed their secondary education in the late 1950s and early 1960s, they shared experience with a public school curriculum that had largely avoided serious consideration of German history from 1918 to 1945. Seeking information on their own about this period, many students were alarmed with their discoveries. As Fritz Ringer has so persuasively demonstrated, the Weimar period levied great stress on a threatened professoriate which on the whole sought to defend itself by belittling established forms of democracy and nostalgically praising earlier, more authoritarian governments.[22] Although not necessarily supporting the National Socialist movement, for the most part the professoriate in 1933 found itself aligned with significant elements of Nazi ideology and in any event placed in a poor position to resist the Nazis.* There-

---

*Perhaps the clearest example of the precarious position of the professoriate is Eduard Spranger, who ultimately resigned his chair in protest against the Nazis. However, in 1932 at a meeting of the *Verband deutscher Universitäten* [*Corporation of German Universities*] he argued against a motion of censure of Nazi student radicals on the

fore, students were able to find many instances of what they regarded as professors clearly collaborating with the Nazi government. As they began to develop their picture of the "brown university" of 1933-45, the students tended to highlight similarities with the university of the mid-1960s, rather than differences.

Gradually the concept of university became for some students a dangerously reactionary instrument reflecting the class structure of an antidemocratic era and capable of manipulation and use by an authoritarian conservative government. In the tradition of such German academic reformers as the founders of the *Burschenshaften* in the early nineteenth century and the revolutionaries of 1848, many idealists among the students believed that by reforming the university it would be possible to reform society itself. Thus, the student impetus for reform took on the urgency of political vision.

In a time of drift away from the ideals of the United States the political vision of the students was influenced by the rediscovery of Germany as a crossroads between East and West, thereby focusing on the conflict between socialist and capitalist models of higher education. This perspective led to a surge of interest and enthusiasm in neo-Marxist models in general and the social philosophers of the "Frankfurt School" in particular. In one of its more constructive forms, the theory that emerged regarded advanced education as capital that should be distributed to society to help promote an egalitarian social structure.[23] Instead of hoarding their intellectual capital by engaging

grounds that "the national movement" was basically genuine, only undisciplined in its expression. See E. Spranger, "Mein Konflikt mit der national-sozialistischen Regierung 1933 ["My Conflict with the National-Socialist Government 1933"], *Universitas: Zeitschrift für Wissenschaft, Kunst und Literatur.*

in obscure research projects for their own limited edification, professors should instead be consciously striving to use their intelligence, training, and facilities to improve the general social welfare.

The "Frankfurt School" was identified principally with the writings of Theodor Adorno, Herbert Marcuse, and Jürgen Habermas. Adorno had taught at the University of Frankfurt until his dismissal by the Nazis and subsequent exile to the United States. He returned in 1949 and headed the philosophy institute at Frankfurt until his death in 1969. The social philosophy associated with Frankfurt began from the simple perspective that educational reform in an advanced capitalistic society is not possible without structural changes. From this premise was developed an elaborate humanistic set of social theories drawing heavily from Hegel, Marx, and Freud, and focusing on the university as a starting point of reform.[24] These cerebral and elegantly drawn neo-Marxist conceptualizations captured the imagination of large numbers of German students in the late 1960s.

One unfortunate element of the neo-Marxist critique of the university was its seeming endorsement of violence as a legitimate instrument of social change. Marcuse, in particular, appeared to defend the concept of violent rebellion against a repressive society. Although violent radicals were never the root cause nor the primary manifestation of the student struggle for reform, the actions of a small group of radicals had important consequences. When revolutionaries bent on violence, particularly at Frankfurt, disrupted classes, destroyed property, and injured professors and others, the university and the society appeared unable to defend itself effectively. Calls for law and order only enhanced the image of a repressive culture. Thus, the disruptive tactics of "crazies" [*Chaoten*] on the fringe sowed the seeds of polarization that made university reform an even more difficult task.

With just a few noble exceptions, established interests within the professoriate who feared that the rapid pace of reform would throw the baby out with the bathwater did little to defend articulately what was widely perceived in the public discussions as a very conservative traditional stance.[25] Instead, pamphleteering activities of professors exploded, and universities and bookstores began to be filled with loosely-reasoned emotional appeals ridiculing cries for democratization and pointing to the chaos that could result from alterations in the status quo. Not atypical of such appeals is the following passage from a widely distributed statement of respected professors adopted at the University of Marburg on 17 April 1968,

> a prominent objection to applying so-called democratization to the university appears to us to be the fact that no other nations of culture, except the Federal Republic and the Peoples Republic of China, have hit upon the idea of "democratizing" so precious and so valuable an institution as the university and its associated organization for teaching and research.[26]

The complete statement of which this passage is a part was eventually publicly endorsed by about 30 percent of the professoriate in the Federal Republic.

University reform efforts that had begun tentatively with open hearings in individual state legislatures in the mid-1960s began to accelerate. In large states where the SPD or an SPD/FDP coalition possessed an absolute majority in the state legislature, such as Hesse and Lower Saxony, comprehensive higher education reform laws were drawn and passed under the supervision of ministers of culture who were themselves reform-minded newcomers to the rank of professor.[27] In the state of Baden-Württemberg, home of such famous German universities as Freiburg, Heidelberg, and Tübingen, a CDU government passed a moderate university-reform law under the guidance of Wilhelm Hahn, a minister of culture who was a clear example of a traditional full professor, a former rector of the University of Heidelberg. There had been a long and sometimes stormy history of efforts at educational reform in Baden-Württemberg, under the early leadership of Kiesinger, Dahrendorf, and others, that resulted in the draft legislation finally passed by the state government in 1968. It is possible that the passage of this law was viewed by some as a political tactic to hold back pressures for serious reform that were building on the horizon.

EIGHT
THE GERMAN UNIVERSITY IN THE FEDERAL REPUBLIC: TURNING TO THE FUTURE, 1970 AND BEYOND

By the time of the federal election of 1969, enough reform laws had been imposed upon universities by state legislatures, and enough reform statutes unilaterally adopted by individual universities, to have generated a widespread sense of a break with the past. It was clear the romantic *Ordinarienuniversität* of Humboldt and Schleiermacher was finally slipping into history and a new university of indeterminate shape was in the initial stages of development. When the newly-formed SPD/FDP national government announced in late 1969 that university reform was at the top of its agenda, amid the tension and excitement that accompanied what to most Germans was a dramatic shift of power, the immediate effect on traditionalists was a sense of panic that brought forth a stern and determined reaction.

Thus in the fall of 1970 a group of established full professors, comprising some of the most famous in Germany, met in Bonn to found an essentially reactionary political pressure organization.* The principal aim of the "Asso-

---

*There were other groups founded as well, some clearly to defend the interests of progressive reform, such as the "Association of Demo-

ciation for Academic Freedom" (*Bund Freiheit der Wissenschaft*) was to protect those elements of the *Ordinarienuniversität* perceived as being essential to the preservation of academic scholarship.[1] A good measure of the alienation of the German professoriate during the period in the late 1960s of rapid change in the universities is the impressive array of scholars who now became members of this association. Many had been identified during the post-war period with issues of university reform, like Helmut Schelsky, Hermann Lübbe, Ernst Nolte, and Wilhelm Hennis, and were now frustrated, disappointed, anxious, and resigned. The reaction spread throughout the Federal Republic wherever a coalition of conservative politicians and anxious professors could have an impact on law, policy, or the communications media. Nowhere, however, was the consequence of this reaction more tragic than in Baden-Württemberg, where a determined minister of culture, fearful that the traditions of such established universities as Heidelberg might be undermined, calculatingly destroyed the one genuinely new liberal reform

---

cratic Scholars" (*Bund demokratischer Wissenschaftler*), but none contained the numbers or the media impact of the Association for Academic Freedom. The adjective 'reactionary' is meant to convey that the Association's purpose grew from reaction to the momentum of university reform initiatives; some might quarrel with this use, but few would deny that the Association's center of gravity lies in the more conservative of Germany's two major political parties. A public opinion survey of German professors reported that 66 percent of those sympathizing with the Association for Academic Freedom vote for CDU politicians; only 8 percent vote for SPD politicians. Among the professoriate as a whole, 17 percent identify themselves as sympathizing with the views of the Association, 33 percent vote for CDU politicians, and 26 percent vote for SPD politicians. W. Sorgel, *Befragung von Lehrenden an Hochschulen, Sommersemester 1974* [*Survey of the Teaching Staff at Universities, Summer Semester, 1974*].

university concept in Germany, the University of Constance.

The idea of a new university to be built in Constance was first proposed during a political conference in Singen in September 1959, by K. G. Kiesinger, then chief executive of the state of Baden-Württemberg. It was just at this time that the *Wissenschaftsrat* was first beginning to address structural issues of university reform, and the Council members who drafted the "stimulative suggestions" for new university patterns kept the possibility in mind that the new university in Constance might be the place to put the suggested reforms into practice. Thus, the bill authorizing establishment of the new university and passed by the Baden-Württemberg legislature on 27 February 1964 contained a phrase indicating that the university proposal had been developed with the help of consultants from the *Wissenschaftsrat*.

The founding commission for the new university, charged with developing preliminary statutes and curriculum plans, was chaired by Gerhard Hess, Professor of Romance Languages, who as president of the German Research Foundation had been instrumental in preparing drafts for university reform within the *Wissenschaftsrat*. Two other key members of the commission were the liberal reformers Waldemar Besson, professor of political science, and Ralf Dahrendorf, professor of sociology. The plan that was developed was cautious, but clearly moved to seek new possibilities for the German university. Students and "middle academics" were represented at every level of decision-making; the rector was to be a committed administrative leader appointed for an indefinite term; the faculty was to be organized by three divisions, groupings were to resemble departments; and new curricula with new degrees, similar to master's degrees, were to be developed. The special character of Constance as an experimental university was given formal recognition by the state when the Baden-Württemberg general university reform law of 1968 exempted Constance from all of its provisions explicitly on grounds of its innovative nature. To insure continuity of the reform idea, Gerhard Hess was appointed rector. The University of Constance was successful in attracting an outstanding faculty and, when it opened its doors in 1966, a talented student body. It acquired the epithet "mini-Harvard on the Lake of Constance" (*klein-Harvard am Bodensee*).

Perhaps one indication of the reform momentum at Constance is that when other German universities started to erupt beginning about 1968 in often violent demonstrations in the cause of university reform, Constance debated these issues fully in its senate and committees, but was otherwise relatively quiet. However, two other Baden-Württemberg universities, Tübingen and Heidelberg, were not quiet, and the serious disturbances at these famous institutions gravely concerned the minister of culture, Wilhelm Hahn.[2] Hahn, a professor of theology whose forebears were famous theologians, ministers, and missionaries, was rector of the University of Heidelberg during 1958-60. He then became active in CDU politics. He served in the national parliament in Bonn, as well as in the state legislature, and was appointed minister of culture for Baden-Württemberg in 1964. After the issue of university reform became highly politicized, and at the time the SPD made this issue one of its leading priorities, Hahn became a rallying point for the conservative reaction. He probably wanted to protect his own university, Heidelberg, from the disintegration he feared would occur if the reforms being undertaken at Constance were permitted to stand and possibly spread throughout

Baden-Württemberg. About six months after formation of the national SPD/FDP government, on 16 June 1970, a colleague of Hahn's, Wolfgang Brezinka, professor of education at Constance, filed a suit in the state court of Baden-Württemberg to have the newly amended statutes of the University of Constance declared null and void.

Like many anxious, now politicized, professors, Brezinka had been active earlier in issues of university reform.[3] Also typical of the alienated mood of the professoriate, Brezinka chose not to express his concern within the agencies of the university, but rather to work to alter the situation by political means external to the university. The matter that concerned both him and Hahn at this moment was the fear that the model of triple parity might establish itself in some form at Constance, be accepted as a legitimate model for other universities, and thereby significantly increase the power of students and middle academics at the expense of the professoriate. Shortly after opening its doors, the University of Constance had amended its statutes so as to elect to its major senate a delegation of forty-five persons in groups of three from within each of the fifteen departments of the university. The three from each department were to include one professor, one middle academic, and one student. To these forty-five were added a variety of *ex-officio* members so that the final composition of the senate was twenty-two professors, sixteen students, sixteen middle academics, two non-academic administrators, and four non-teaching professional staff. Because the tradition of dependence upon the state in Germany requires state approval of all university statutes, the amendments had been approved by Hahn on behalf of the state government.

On 25 November 1971, the state court did in fact declare the statues null and void, not for any of the reasons argued by Brezinka, but on a subtle technicality. The court found the statutes invalid because the letter of the law required that the amendments go through the formal procedure of decree by the state government rather than the procedure of approval. Because they had been approved, but not decreed, the statutes had not legally taken effect. The Court suggested the simple remedy of decree. Hahn chose not to exercise this solution. Instead, he ordered that the University of Constance be governed by a senate composed solely of full professors while the Ministry of Culture decided how to proceed.

The election of the state government occurred during this period when the university was without statutes. During the election campaign the Ministry of Culture often repeated that the triple parity statutes at Constance could not be reconstituted. In fact, the senate that was declared invalid at Constance only indirectly involved a principal of triple parity, had no relation to the triple parity models that had become the heart of much reform ideology, was freely and independently developed to meet the special situation at Constance, and contained a greater proportion of full professors than any other represented group. Gerhard Hess worked patiently and unstintingly to arrive at least at some temporary solution, but Hahn was unyielding. Of the three major figures at the founding of the university, Hess was now alone: Besson had recently died and Dahrendorf had left the university to become active in FDP politics. Besson had had particularly good relations with the CDU politicians in the state capital of Stuttgart, and his absence during this crisis was sorely felt. Students and faculty at the university grew impatient not only with Hahn, but also with Hess's patience.

In this tense atmosphere, Professor Brezinka wrote Hahn a letter asking whether, in light of the court's decision, it was still appropriate for students to continue to sit on committees within academic departments. Hahn replied formally and directly to Hess that the answer to Brezinka's question was that students were not permitted to sit on such committees. Thus, within a six month period, students were summarily removed from representation on all but one small committee of the university by state action, against the expressed deliberations of the university itself. In late May 1972, the first serious student demonstrations ever held in Constance occurred to protest these destructive unilateral actions by the state government. Hahn responded on 9 June 1972 by releasing a set of statutes for the University of Constance prepared entirely within the Ministry of Culture. The statutes dealt not only with the matter of the senate, but also with every aspect of what was considered important at Constance: the structure and governance of academic departments, methods of voting, responsibilities of various agencies, etc. Both Gerhard Hess, the rector, and Horst Sund, professor of biology and prorector, resigned. Hess offered to continue functioning as rector if Hahn would agree to negotiate over the statutes. Hahn agreed, but was then unwilling to make any concessions during the negotiations.

On 27 September Hess took the ministry's statutes to the senate of full professors and asked for advice. A substantial majority voted to reject them and directed the rector to reenter negotiations. Accordingly, Hess sought new negotiations. On 17 October Hahn unilaterally imposed the statutes. Hess stepped down immediately, and no one at the university was prepared to assume leadership. Hahn met this situation by appointing a CDU politician, Theopont Diez, a member of the state legislature since 1953, as acting rector of the university. Diez had no academic credentials and possessed the sole administrative qualification of having been a long-time mayor of the town of Singen. The new statutes imposed upon Constance by the Ministry of Culture brought the university into line with all other universities in Baden-Württemberg. By this calculated act, the one most promising laboratory for university reform in the Federal Republic was imperiously and summarily removed.[4]

The utter dependence of the university upon the state in Germany is revealed by this sad episode, as well as the illusory nature of academic freedom in Germany. Not only are governing statutes subject to formal state approval, but individual faculty appointments as well. For example, in 1973 the University of Constance sought to fill the full professorship once held by Waldemar Besson with the appointment of a well-known leftist and critic of the United States, Ekkehart Krippendorf. Abiding by the statutes provided by the ministry, Krippendorf was elected to the chair by a search committee, confirmed by the department of political science, by a major senate, and by a minor senate of the university. The recommendation for appointment was then sent routinely to the ministry. Hahn rejected the appointment summarily, defending his actions by producing an anonymous evaluation which characterized Krippendorf's scholarly work as "journalistic," and directed the university to produce a more acceptable candidate.

It is not the loss of the specific faculty member that is illustrative, but rather a process that summarily ignores and thwarts academic judgment without consultation. The aristocratic heritage of the university is at work here. One might say that as long as the minister of culture is wise, in accord with the nineteenth century ideal that Humboldt promoted, the university is protected and capable of greatness. However, under unenlightened stewardship it is vulnerable and subject to crippling damage.

The perceptible reaction to university reform was further highlighted when the Federal Constitutional Court finally issued its ruling on the suit against triple parity filed by the law professors at the University of Göttingen. On 29 May 1973, the court ruled in favor of the professors. Deciding solely on the basis of the sentence "research and teaching are free," the court handed down a lengthy opinion which in effect constituted guidelines for the governing structure of universities.[5] Although there were six principal points in the decision, the critical judgment was that professors must be given at least 51 percent of the vote in any committee or agency that has authority in academic or research matters. The court did not specify that the professors must be full professors, only that the grouping of professors must be homogeneous, thus leaving open the possibility that junior professors and middle academics could be counted among the professors who are to constitute at least 51 percent.

One vignette during the period of reaction was the demise of the "Frankfurt School." At the height of student unrest, between 1968-70, radical student leftists turned upon the founding father, Theodor Adorno, accusing him of staying intellectually above the real revolution and thus of being a bourgeois defender of the social status quo. Just before he died, Adorno issued a statement warning against attempts to achieve university reform "through Molotov cocktails and violence."[6] Many students viewed his statement as a defense of purely theoretical work in the tradition of the university's abstract search for truth. Since by implication Adorno's work was never meant actually to be put into practice, as the students were now attempting to do, his statement had the effect of discrediting him with many of the students he had inspired. Threatened by leftist violence, his last set of final examinations at Frankfurt before his death had to be held under police surveillance. Herbert Marcuse had never returned to Frankfurt from the United States and remained in retirement in San Diego. Jürgen Habermas eventually left the students and the university for a pure research position at a Max Planck Institute in a rural area of Bavaria. The Frankfurt School simply ceased to exist.

During the period of rapid reform in the late 1960s a set of amendments to the federal constitution was passed in 1969 that permitted federal involvement with the planning and financing of the universities. The amendments also authorized the federal government to pass a coordinating law for universities (*Hochschulrahmengesetz*) which would set a general national standard for structure and function of the university system. A draft proposal of such a law was one of the first documents submitted by the new SPD/FDP government to the legislature in June 1970. The bill focused on five priorities: (*a*) Amalgamation of various types of higher educational institutions, *e.g.*, technical universities, teacher-training colleges and universities, into one coordinated comprehensive university (*die Gesamthochschule*); (*b*) development of specified curricula, with stated examinations and recommended completion times, for each academic discipline; (*c*) reorganization of the academic personnel structure into departments containing groups of professors and assistant professors who work together; (*d*) statute guidelines to insure participation of students and middle academics on matters that affect them, such as curriculum design; (*e*) more efficient means of administration, including replacement of the institution of rotating rectors with more permanent presidents.

Unfortunately, the draft federal coordinating law was proposed just at the time when the reaction to university reform was hardening within the CDU/CSU, which continued to control the upper house of parliament (*Bundesrat*). After lengthy tedious debate that spanned more than two years, and numerous alterations in the text, the bill was defeated on three consecutive occasions by a large majority in the upper house, with more than fifty motions for change still pending on the floor at the time of the third vote. Its principal author, Hans Leussink, former rector of the Technical University of Karlsruhe, and chairman of the *Wissenschaftsrat* from 1965-9, then resigned his position as federal minister for higher education. He was replaced by a skilled politician, Klaus von Dohnanyi, who had studied law at Munich, Columbia, and Stanford, receiving his LL.B. from Yale. Dohnanyi had been a member of the SPD since 1957, and a member of parliament representing the federal ministry for higher education and research since formation of the national government in 1969. He vowed to try again, adopting a more pragmatic approach.

The new proposed federal coordinating law was drafted during a process of elaborate and thorough consultation with virtually every political interest group that represented a significant body of opinion. The result was an elegantly crafted, fair, and balanced legislative proposal which was unanimously endorsed by the federal cabinet on 29 August 1973. However, by this time the CDU/CSU sensed a major shift in public opinion in its favor and was in no mood to compromise; CDU/CSU representatives in the upper house of parliament began to introduce amendments that would have had the effect of returning to the status quo of about 1965. At the same time, students and younger professors to the left of the political spectrum began to attack such provisions in the bill as the requirements for structured curricula as an assault on academic freedom. The bill foundered, Minister Dohnanyi began to look uncomfortable, and when Chancellor Schmidt succeeded Brandt in the Spring of 1974 Dohnanyi was replaced as minister by a quiet non-academic politician with a reputation for effective service, Helmut Rohde.

Rohde guided the bill to the floor of the lower house, controlled by the SPD/FDP coalition, and encouraged conciliatory minor amendments on the floor of the house. The bill passed the lower house in late 1974 and was then forwarded to the upper house, controlled by the CDU/CSU, which rejected it, thereby bringing into play a joint negotiating committee of the two houses. The negotiating committee was chaired by a former minister of justice for the SPD, Gerhard Jahn, who, like Rohde, was prepared for the realistic and hard negotiating necessary to obtain a politically acceptable compromise.[7]

Although many emotional ideological issues appeared to be at stake, the real crux of the negotiations revolved around the extent to which universities and other post-secondary educational institutions would be forced by law to conform to a general national model. All parties agreed that a certain degree of conformity was desirable; the disagreement was over whether the national model itself would be dictated by the SPD/FDP. Therefore, a major goal of the CDU/CSU was to retain as much control over details for the individual states as possible, at the expense of federal conformity, so that universities in CDU or CSU states could retain and develop more traditional models. Finally, in early December 1975 a compromise was reached in the committee that permitted Hans Maier, a prominent CSU intellectual and minister of culture for the State of Bavaria, to declare, "On Thursday of last week the course set by the CDU/CSU clearly established itself."[8] After passage by both houses, the federal coordinating law for universities was officially decreed by the government on 26 January 1976. The individual states were given three years beyond this date to bring state laws into conformity with the new federal law.

Although the federal coordinating law permits the states to retain significant power of individuation over university purpose and structure, it also introduces for the first time considerable legal uniformity among universities throughout the Federal Republic. In fact many of the "reforms" had gradually been implemented at the state level during the intense six-year negotiations over the new law. With respect to the initial five priorities set by the SPD/FDP in 1970, the outcome was as follows: (*a*) Universities within states are to coordinate their activities with all other post-secondary educational institutions, but they are free to choose between integrated coordination, in which links between the institutions will be organic and functional, or cooperative coordination, in which links will be primarily consultative. The former model (*die integrierte Gesamthochschule*) was championed by the SPD/FDP, the latter (*die kooperative Gesamthochschule*) by the CDU/CSU. (*b*) Each discipline at each university is to establish curricula which permit students to take an examination for the first university degree no later than four years after matriculation. Unless a special case justifies a particular extension, students will be required to take the examination at the stated time, usually four years after matriculation, or lose their status as students altogether. (*c*) The basic organizational unit of the university becomes a disciplinary department (*Fachbereich*), to be headed by an elected department chairman (*Fachbereichssprecher*), who must be a professor. Thus, departments replace institutes, and collections of professors working together replace the authority of a single *Ordinarius*. (*d*) Academic committees must be composed of four groups: professors, students, professional assistants and specialists, and "other" professionals. However, professors must constitute at least 51 percent of all such committees. Further, in all matters involving curriculum, academic expenditures, or searches for new professors, a majority of the professors on the committee must concur before a decision is valid. Professors are treated as a homogeneous grouping, consisting of junior professors with a somewhat lower rate of pay (the C-2 and C-3 pay scales) as well as senior professors with a higher rate of pay (the C-4 pay scale). Young academics with doctoral degrees just beginning their academic careers are specifically excluded from the grouping of professors; they are called assistants (*Hochschulassistenten*), grouped with professional assistants and specialists. They may be appointed to a three-year term, renewable only once, for a total maximum of six years of service. If within these six years they have not been called to a professorship they must then unconditionally leave the university. (*e*) Universities must be headed by a full-time administrator elected by the university, and approved by the state, for a four-year renewable term. This administrator replaces the traditional rector who was a professor elected by other professors and who continued to teach and do research while serving as head of the university. However, a form of the traditional rectorate governance is permitted in those states which choose to have universities run by councils, providing that at least one member of the council, the nominal head, is a full-time administrator. It is anticipated that where this option is chosen, the council will be similar to the traditional academic senate consisting of present and former rectors and deans.

The state of the university in the Federal Republic of Germany just after passage of the federal coordinating law in the late 1970s consisted of a considerable diversity of ideas and institutions. There were well known giant universities (Munich, Hamburg, Münster), and small ones (Constance, Augsburg, Bremen); traditional ones (Freiburg, Göttingen) and those seeking identity (Regensburg, Trier, Bielefeld); quiet ones (Cologne, Kiel) and noisy ones (Berlin, Frankfurt); there were states where full professors maintained traditional authority (Bavaria, Schleswig-Holstein), and others where authority was held in check by students and post-doctoral assistants (Berlin, Bremen, Hesse).[9] Although violence and disruption at universities by leftist radicals was widely reported in Germany in the 1970s, these reports focused on four institutions with unique past histories and contemporary circumstances: Berlin, Bremen, Frankfurt, and Marburg. As the German educational commentator Rudolf Leonhardt pointed out, setting aside press coverage from these four universities reduces the reports of leftist trouble by about 90 percent.[10] In fact, toward the late 1970s the revolutionary atmosphere among students in Germany, just as in the U.S., had been largely replaced by an emphasis on serious study.[11]

Although the purpose of the federal coordinating law was to create a certain uniformity and adherence to a set of common general principles among universities in the Federal Republic of Germany, perhaps its most important effect was to show the extent to which differentiation was possible. As a result the diversity of universities in

Germany was enhanced rather than inhibited by the law. By requiring each state in the Federal Republic to write its own specific university law in conformity with the general provisions of the federal law, the federal law in effect encouraged state governments to write laws that protected what they felt were the special features of the universities in their states. Thus, by 1980 although general tenets of university reform were universally established throughout the Federal Republic, the differentiation in organization, style, and emphasis among universities was truly startling relative to 1960.

Throughout the 1970s, as in the beginnings of the university crisis some fifteen years earlier, the debate on university purpose and structure continued to be dominated by overwhelming quantitative considerations. The number of students seeking university study exceeded the available spaces so severely that students who achieved the *Abitur* faced restrictions on entry to virtually all fields of study. These restrictions, called generically *Numerus Clausus*, make admission contingent upon such factors as intended major field of study, actual score on the *Abitur*, number of years on a waiting list for admission to study at the university, professional experience, and parental occupation and income. In such health-related fields as dentistry and pharmacy, a student who passed the *Abitur* in some instances had to wait an average of six years before gaining entry to study at a university.[12]

The introduction of the *Numerus Clausus* as a restriction on entry to the university is a significant break with the Humboldtian tradition that anyone who successfully passes the *Abitur* gains immediate access to the full resources of the university. Nonetheless, the *Numerus Clausus* seems destined to become a standard element of German university life because of continued demand for entry and realistic limits of growth. By the time the federal coordinating law had been passed, the highly productive postwar economy of the Federal Republic had begun to slow down, and university education was known to entail astronomical public costs. For example, in 1973 public expenditures per university student in the Federal Republic amounted to more than 100,000 DM.[13] Such costs, combined with anxieties about the prospect of widespread unemployment among university graduates, began to inhibit university growth in the late 1970s. The phrase "academic proletariat" began to appear with some frequency in discussions of university expansion.[14] In fact, by 1980 an increasingly large number of potential students who had passed the *Abitur* had decided to forego university study altogether and enter the work force directly.

All of the principal problems that dominated the debate in the 1970s over higher education in the Federal Republic revolve around the central social phenomenon of adaptation to mass education at the university level. It is important to keep in mind that the university, including the technical university, is just one of several kinds of higher education institutions in Germany. The others include teacher-training colleges (*Pädagogische Hochschulen*), specialized colleges (*Fachhochschulen*), and various technical and vocational colleges. From 1950 to 1973 all such institutions expanded by about 400 percent at equivalent rates. In 1950, there were 116,900 students in universities, and in 1973 there were 485,500. In 1950, there were 57,100 students in all other institutions of higher education; in 1973 there were 228,600. There were thus a total of 714,100 higher education students in 1973. 1974 was the first year that more than 20 percent of the appropriate age group (generally 19-23 year-olds) entered some form of higher education in the Federal Republic.[15]

The enlightenment university of Humboldt and Schleiermacher, heroic as it was, was designed specifically for an elite. Among universities in the Federal Republic in 1960, there was no hierarchical pyramid of more elite to less elite institutions; they were all equally elite, and inextricably linked by tradition. Thus, it was not possible for some to change mission and purpose without all being affected, and the enlightenment tradition on which they were all based was poorly suited to the education of broad masses in the social structure.[16] Yet, mass higher education is essential to modern industrial nations, and the challenge of adapting the Federal Republic to mass higher education was the source of the difficulty for the German university. In the end, it was impossible for the enlightenment university of Humboldt and Schleiermacher to survive this challenge. The elegant institution that persisted into the 1950s was thus washed away in the two following decades.

NINE
CONCLUSION

The period of dramatic reform for the contemporary German university has peaked and passed. There is little question that the enlightenment university developed by Humboldt and Schleiermacher no longer exists in the clear form that held sway for 150 years, and there is at present no agreement on a single new model to replace it. In the mid-1970s the German university entered a phase of development and consolidation that will continue actively for some time. It is unlikely that totally new ideas of university purpose and structure will appear in the foreseeable future. Rather, the intense and earnest debate of the period between 1960 and 1980 articulated virtually all of the principal reform possibilities. What will occur in the coming years is a gradual sifting and sorting of these possibilities; some will find fertile soil and take hold, others will wither and be discarded. In this process, the profile of a new German university will emerge.

Some of the elements of a new profile are already clearly visible in the near-universal acceptance of some of the reforms adopted at various moments between 1960 and 1980. For example, the professoriate has become more heterogeneous, more flexible, more prone to permit the healthy conflict of competing ideas. In the Federal Republic the significance of a senior professorship is now somewhat simply associated with a scale of pay in recognition of intellectual achievement. Junior professors have virtually all of the rights and privileges of senior professors, but are rewarded with a lower scale of pay appropriate to their intellectual level of development. The formal process of *Habilitation* is no longer an absolute prerequisite to holding a professorship, but rather a scholar's worth is now more often measured directly by the quality of the candidate's continuing scholarship. The rational integration of junior professors into the professoriate has greatly ameliorated the traditional isolation of the former *Nichtordinarien.*

Postdoctoral assistants aspiring to professorial careers are now typically given standard renewable contracts to a maximum of six years, after which they are expected to assume a professorship or move on to some other career. To reduce an earlier form of exploitation of these assistants, the federal coordinating law requires that they be appropriately cited by professors who publish research to which assistants have contributed. Paradoxically, the rapid expansion of universities during the 1960s, coupled with the limits on growth in the 1970s, produced the unanticipated side effect of making professorships less accessible to developing young scholars. This is because professorships carrying tenure were filled as rapidly as they were created in the 1960s so that such positions are now being held in large numbers by young professors who will not vacate them for thirty years or more. Out of concern that the six-year maximum specified in the federal coordinating law might result in the permanent loss of some of the most promising scholars, by 1980 several state governments were creating new "limited-term" professorships as holding positions for the best of those assistants who had come to the end of the six years.[1]

It is now universal custom, required by the federal coordinating law, to advertise every open professorship widely, and for aspiring candidates to apply for whatever position they believe themselves to be qualified. This seemingly simple reform has resulted in an extremely important change by opening university positions to the full range of intellectual talent and reducing the abusive caprice of personal influence by a few full professors in filling vacant professorships. Because there are more professors in a discipline, and the range of views is greater, the monopolistic control of academic disciplines by single full professors has been broken. Universities have moved toward a pattern of organization by academic department, in which all concerned with a given discipline are grouped together and share academic authority.

Student voices are now being heard and responded to, particularly on matters of curriculum planning. The result is more frequent evaluative information, including formal examinations, better academic advice, and a more differentiated and clearer degree structure. The intricate interplay of research, teaching, and learning has become more sophisticated, and new roles of professor and student are developing within this complex web. One feature of the federal coordinating law, the provision for curricula to be completed within a fixed period of time, helped to focus attention on the plight of students subjected to uncoordinated curricula and unsystematically scheduled examinations related only loosely to the curricula. However, this provision proved to be the most controversial feature of the law and was the first element to be changed through amendment, in February, 1980. Unpopular with both faculty and students, the provision instead of motivating students tended to unsteady them. Faculty argued further that examinations forced at an arbitrary point worked against a carefully structured educational plan.[2] The amendment retains coordinated curricula and timely completion of a degree as a goal, but removes explicit penalties for not completing a degree in a fixed period of time.

Means of admission to the university other than the *Abitur* are becoming available to a broader array of students from more varied socio-economic backgrounds. The West German Conference of University Rectors proposed in 1974 that the *Abitur* be phased out and some alternative admissions process be developed.[3] These developments in admissions, along with the continuing *Numerus Clausus,* are important evidence that gradually a new conception of higher education is emerging in Germany.

Finally, and most important, it must be stressed that universities are exceptionally well supported in the Federal Republic of Germany. Research equipment, space, support staff, and faculty salaries are unquestionably among the best in the world.[4] It is surely a mark of strength that the crisis which so profoundly hit the German university in the 1960s was met forthrightly. The implementation of the reforms which are in the process of transforming universities throughout the Federal Republic has been accomplished with determination and with confidence in the strength and purpose of these institutions. It is remarkable that although the numbers of students increased dramatically between 1960 and the late 1970s, on balance, the number of professors and support staff increased in even greater numbers, thereby greatly strengthening the universities. On a scale in which students, professors, and support staff each were at 100 in

1960, by 1976 students were at 212, but professors were at 433, and support staff at 314.[5]

In drawing a balance of progress versus reaction since 1960 it is clear that progress and change have been dominant. The steady stream of thoughtful proposals from the moderate *Wissenschaftsrat* contributed to successful reform, but the truly significant event, the defined turning point to the future, was the successful passage of a compromise federal coordinating law. The law represents a public compact that universities can be strengthened and reformed at the same time. Such progress could not have been accomplished if universities had been considered weak in 1960, nor if there had not been significant sympathy for reform. Although reform efforts on a national scale did not appear to mobilize until 1969, the basic principles of university reform can be viewed as developing gradually but steadily since 1945. In 1969 these principles began to break through in public policy. In effect, universities became genuinely part of the body politic. Thereafter, university reform can be viewed as a continuing public process in the Federal Republic of Germany.

The proud heroic German university on the model of Berlin, 1810, has disappeared. Although its structure was recreated almost perfectly between 1945 and 1960, the nineteenth-century flower could not take root in twentieth-century soil. A romantic university of heroes, asserting human intellect with daring self confidence, has come to terms with an antiheroic era where the wisdom of experience has made of self confidence vice rather than virtue. As the processes of twentieth-century intellect have made an alien of the concept of hero, so was the Humboldtian university in the Federal Republic in 1960 symbolic of an alienated hero. That university is gone. Still, in passing, it transmitted its essential enduring values to a modern world. Driven by energy radiated from those values, and confident in their promise, the determination and intelligence necessary to build a vigorous new university remains in Germany.

NOTES

Chapter One

1. A. L. Cross, "The University of Michigan in Ann Arbor, 1837-1937," in W. B. Shaw, ed., *A University Between Two Centuries*; S. B. Schurtz, "The First Twenty Years," in Shaw, ed., *A University*; and E. E. Slosson, *Great American Universities*. See also W. C. De Vane, *Higher Education in Twentieth Century America*, chaps. 1-3. For a brief informed description of the influence of the German university on U.S. higher education, with references to some of the most important sources on this topic, see R. Hofstadter and W. P. Metzger, *The Development of Academic Freedom in the United States*, pp. 367-412.

2. G. S. Hall, "Educational Reforms," *The Pedagogical Seminary*, pp. 6-8.

3. A. Flexner, *Universities: American, English, German*, p. 315.

4. Personal communication from Mr. Conant, 12 October 1974. Also cited in W. Meyer-Erlach, "The Cultural Scene in Germany Today," in J. P. Payne, ed., *Germany Today: Introductory Studies*, p. 158.

5. C. Kerr, "Introduction: The Evaluation of National Systems of Higher Education," in B. B. Burn, ed., *Higher Education in Nine Countries,* pp. 5-6.

6. An informative and valuable comparison of elementary and secondary education systems in the Federal Republic of Germany and the German Democratic Republic from 1945 to 1970 is available in A. Hearndon, *Education in the Two Germanies.* A similar description of education in the German Democratic Republic which touches briefly on universities is M. J. Moore-Rinvolucri, *Education in East Germany.*

Chapter Two

1. F. Paulsen, *Geschichte des gelehrten Unterrichts. Erster Band* [*The History of Scholarly Instruction, I*], p. 524. See also F. Lilge, *The Abuse of Learning,* p. 3.

2. *"die im Zunftwesen erstarrte Universität."* See H. Schelsky, *Einsamkeit und Freiheit* [*Solitude and Freedom*], p. 21.

3. R. S. Turner, "University Reformers and Professorial Scholarship in Germany 1760-1806," in L. Stone, ed., *The University in Society.*

4. Schelsky, *Einsamkeit und Freiheit,* pp. 20-30.

5. Paulsen, *Geschichte I,* describes on pp. 535-50 the founding of the University of Halle, calling it the first modern university in the world and its founding one of the most significant events in the history of universities. See also Schelsky, *Einsamkeit und Freiheit,* p. 19. Also F. Paulsen, *Geschichte des gelehrten Unterrichts, Zweiter Band* [*The History of Scholarly Instruction, II*], on the founding and character of the University of Göttingen, pp. 9-46; on the intellectual period of Weimar-Jena, pp. 200-4.

6. F. K. Ringer, *The Decline of the German Mandarins,* p. 21. See also Lilge, *Abuse,* pp. 37-8.

7. R. König, *Vom Wesen der deutschen Universität* [*From the Spirit of the German University*], pp. 49-53.

8. Lilge, *Abuse,* p. 5.

9. A concise account of this period and the role played in it by Beyme can be found in Schelsky, *Einsamkeit und Freiheit,* pp. 42-5. See also M. Lenz, *Geschichte der Königlichen Friedrich-Wilhelms-Universität zu Berlin. Band I* [*History of the Royal Frederick William University in Berlin, I*], pp. 24-70.

10. *"Das ist recht, das ist brav! Der Staat muss durch geistige Kräfte ersetzen, was er an physischen verloren hat."* E. Spranger, "Gedenkrede zur 150-Jahrfeier der Gründung der Friedrich-Wilhelms Universität in Berlin" ["Memorial Lecture on the Occasion of the 150th Anniversary Celebration of the Founding of the Frederick William University in Berlin"], in H. Rothfels, ed., *Berlin in Vergangenheit und Gegenwart, Tübinger Vorträge* [*Berlin, Past and Present, the Tübingen Lectures*], see p. 62. See also H. Lübbe, "Mythos oder Modell? Humboldts preussische Universitätsreform" ["Myth or Model? Humboldt's Prussian University Reform"], *Hamburger Sonntagsblatt.* Also Schelsky, *Einsamkeit und Freiheit,* p. 46, and Lenz, *Geschichte Universität Berlin,* p. 78.

Chapter Three

1. J. H. Knoll, "Vater der Universität: Zum 200. Geburtstag Wilhelm v. Humboldts" ["Father of the University: On the Occasion of the 200th Birthday of Wilhelm von Humboldt"], *Die Welt.*

2. Lübbe, "Mythos oder Modell?"

3. A recent text published in the German Democratic Republic contains the following introductory statement: "The Humboldt University in Berlin originated in the strivings of patriotic and humanistic forces in the time of the struggle against foreign Napoleonic domination, and in the execution of bourgeois reforms. However, the philosophical premises of the founder of the university, Wilhelm von Humboldt, which were to create a unity of teaching, research, and cultivation of character in the service of historical progress, can only first truly be realized and brought further onto a new level in a socialist society." K. H. Wirzberger, *Die Humboldt-Universität zu Berlin* [*The Humboldt University in Berlin*], p. 5. In accordance with prevailing custom the University of Berlin was named after the reigning monarch at the time of its founding. Thus, its official name was the *Königliche Friedrich-Wilhelms-Universität zu Berlin* (Royal Frederick William University in Berlin). Since 1949, the same buildings have carried the name of *Humboldt-Universität zu Berlin* (Humboldt University in Berlin).

4. The most important essays relating to the idea of the new university are collected in E. Anrich, ed., *Die Idee der deutschen Universität* [*The Idea of the German University*].

5. W. von Humboldt, "Über die innere und äussere Organization der höheren wissenschaftlichen Anstalten zu Berlin" ["Concerning the Internal and External Organization of the Higher Scientific Establishments of Berlin"], in E. Anrich, ed., *Idee,* pp. 375-86. This brief section of what is assumed to have been a longer essay appeared for the first time in print in B. Gebhardt, *Wilhelm von Humboldt als Staatsmann. Band I* [*Wilhelm von Humboldt as Statesman, I*], pp. 118-24. Gebhardt found this fragment in Humboldt's own handwriting in a file drawer in the Prussian Academy of Arts and Sciences. It was probably part of a working memorandum.

6. An account of Humboldt's reluctance is described in König, *Wesen*, p. 151. See also Lenz, *Geschichte Universität Berlin*, pp. 153-6.

7. A relatively thorough description of Humboldt's activities during his sixteen months as director of the section for culture and public instruction of the Ministry of the Interior can be found in Gebhardt, *Humboldt*, pp. 95-368. See also Lenz, *Geschichte Universität Berlin*, pp. 148-219; E. Spranger, *Wilhelm von Humboldt und die Humanitätsidee* [*Wilhelm von Humboldt and the Humanitarian Idea*]; E. Spranger, *Wilhelm von Humboldt und die Reform des Bildungswesens* [*Wilhelm von Humboldt and Academic Reform*].

8. M. Farrand, *The Framing of the Constitution of the United States*.

9. *Ideen zu einem Versuch die Grenzen der Wirksamkeit des Staates zu Bestimmen*. The essay is also known by the English translation of Joseph Coulthart (London, 1854), whose translation of the title is simply "The Sphere and Duties of Government."

10. H. Hahne, "Gegenwart im Dasein: Wilhelm von Humboldt, geboren am 22. Juni 1767." ["Presence through Existence: Wilhelm von Humboldt, born on 22 June 1767"], *Frankfurter allgemeine Zeitung*.

11. N. Chomsky, *Cartesian Linguistics*, p. 2; for a discussion of Humboldt's particular original contributions to modern linguistics, see also p. 22.

12. E. P. Cubberley, *The History of Education*, pp. 562-3. See also H. G. Good and J. D. Teller, *A History of Western Education*, p. 348.

13. H. Krüsi, *Pestalozzi: His Life, Work, and Influence*, pp. 202-12; Gebhardt, *Humboldt*, pp. 278-9.

14. The most important sections of Humboldt's proposals for these two school systems are reprinted in G. Giese, *Quellen zur deutschen Schulgeschichte seit 1800* [*Sources for German Educational History Since 1800*]. The Königsberg school plan is described on pp. 64-71 and the Lithuanian school plan on pp. 71-3, with a brief general discussion of both of these on pp. 16-19.

15. Humboldt, "Organization," p. 381 (first quotation), pp. 377-8 (second quotation).

16. Cubberley, *History of Education*, pp. 572-3, describes the first reform accurately and succinctly as follows: "In 1810 the examination of all secondary-school teachers, according to a uniform state plan, was ordered. The examinations were to be conducted for the State by the university authorities; to be based on university training in the gymnasial subjects, with an opportunity to reveal secondary preparation in any subject or subjects; and no one in the future could even be nominated as a gymnasial teacher who had not passed this examination."

17. Gebhardt, *Humboldt*, p. 233. See also Cubberley, *History of Education*, pp. 464-5, 573-4 and Paulsen, *Geschichte II*, pp. 289-90.

18. Humboldt, "Organization," p. 380 (both quotations).

19. Spranger, "Gedenkrede," p. 65.

20. The negotiations with Wolf are delightfully described in Lenz, *Geschichte Universität Berlin*, pp. 157-9, 208-10, 267-9. See also Schelsky, *Einsamkeit und Freiheit*, pp. 45-6, 118.

21. The particular selection of important figures among the inaugural faculty is mine. Similar but lengthier listings covering

a broader time span have been made by Lübbe, "Mythos oder Modell?," and P. Binswanger, *Wilhelm von Humboldt*, p. 242. A complete description of negotiations for the inaugural faculty, including accounts of those with scholars who declined overtures, is contained in Lenz, *Geschichte Universität Berlin*, pp. 161-276; the dates cited are from Lenz, pp. 175, 191, and 211, as is the report of Humboldt's dealings with Gauss, pp. 205-6. On Gauss, see also Binswanger, *ibid.*, p. 242.

22. Spranger, "Gedenkrede," p. 64.

23. Lenz, *Geschichte Universität Berlin*, pp. 188-95.

24. F. Rudolph, *The American College and University: A History*, pp. 42, 124-8, 107-12. See also A. Fried, ed., *The Essential Jefferson*, pp. 149-55, 527-32.

25. Lenz, *Geschichte Universität Berlin*, pp. 171-5, 191-3, 314-16.

26. R. Dahrendorf, *Society and Democracy in Germany*, especially pp. 188-203.

27. Lilge, *Abuse*, p. 10.

28. Humboldt, "Organization," p. 379.

29. Humboldt, "Organization," p. 385.

30. The quotations from these letters were selected by Lenz, *Geschichte Universität Berlin*, p. 210. See also Schelsky, *Einsamkeit und Freiheit*, p. 119.

31. On 11 Aug. 1813 the professor of medicine K. A. Rudolphi was easily elected rector by the faculty of full professors for the next term, which he served well without incident. The entertaining story of the first balloting is recounted in Lenz, *Ge-*

schichte Universität Berlin, pp. 318, 399-400; other dates and incidents, pp. 402, 431, 521. See also Schelsky, *Einsamkeit und Freiheit,* pp. 51-2.

32. J. G. Fichte, "Deduzierter Plan einer in Berlin zu errichtenden höheren Lehranstalt" ["A Deduced Plan for an Institution of Higher Education to be Established in Berlin"], in Anrich, ed., *Idee,* pp. 124-218. See also Spranger, "Gedenkrede," p. 63.

33. The title of his speech, which established the reputation of Halle as a free and enlightened university, was *De libertate Fridericianae: die Friedrichsuniversität das atrium libertatis. Was ist die Aufgabe der Universität?* [*On Frederician Liberty: King Frederick's University as Liberty's Atrium: What is the Purpose of the University?*], Paulsen, *Geschichte I,* pp. 543-4. See also Cubberley, *History of Education,* p. 554.

34. Lübbe, "Mythos oder Modell?"

Chapter Four

1. F. E. D. Schleiermacher, "Gelegentliche Gedanken über Universitäten im deutschen Sinn" ["Opportune Thoughts on Universities in the German Sense"], in Anrich, ed., *Idee,* pp. 219-308. The modifying phrase "in the German sense" expressed a sentiment of resistance against the French occupation of Prussia and most of Germany, and underscored rejection of the Napoleonic principle of centralization of authority. See Spranger, "Gedenkrede," p. 64.

2. This usage follows Ringer, *Mandarins,* pp. 35-6, who also comments on titles for less central positions, such as *ausserplanmässiger, nichtetatsmässiger, persönlicher, titular,* and *honorar* professor.

3. Lenz, *Geschichte Universität Berlin*, pp. 287, 356. Lenz says that the large number of students representative of the higher social classes was indeed remarkable. There were twenty sons of high civil servants, ten of high-ranking military officers, and thirty-two of nobility.

4. Lenz, *Geschichte Universität Berlin*, pp. 161-276; Paulsen, *Geschichte II*, p. 250.

5. The entire discussion in the text on the development of the statutes relies heavily on the detailed account provided by Lenz, *Geschichte Universität Berlin:* for Humboldt's original commission which prepared the provisional statutes, pp. 211, 220, 277-9, 287; the negation of hierarchy within the professorial rank, p. 225; the neutralization of the provisional statutes, p. 314; the new four-professor advisory commission and the drafting of permanent statutes, pp. 432-4; the senate, pp. 445-6; the concept of the rector as *primus inter pares*, pp. 445, 447-9; final approval of the permanent statutes, pp. 632-5.

Chapter Five

1. Lenz, *Geschichte Universität Berlin*, pp. 259, 461.

2. Ringer, *Mandarins*, p. 32. F. Paulsen, *Die deutschen Universitäten und das Universitätsstudium* [*The German Universities and University Study*], pp. 435-41. This work is available in a good English translation by F. Thilly and W. W. Elang as F. Paulsen, *The German Universities and University Study*.

3. Schleiermacher, "Gelegentliche Gedanken."

4. Lenz, *Geschichte Universität Berlin*, pp. 280, 458-9.

5. Ringer, *Mandarins*, pp. 37-8.

6. Paulsen, *Universitäten*, pp. 102-4.

7. Ringer, *Mandarins*, p. 54.

8. H. Walther, "Die Revolution des Jahres 1848 und die Reform der Universitäten in Deutschland" ["The Revolution of 1848 and University Reform in Germany"], *Freiburger Universitätsblätter.*

9. Paulsen, *Geschichte II*, pp. 707-8.

10. Gebhardt, *Humboldt*, pp. 103-4. See also Lilge, *Abuse*, p. 23. For a comprehensive collection of documents and essays that traces the important historical development of student organizations in Germany, particularly the *Burschenschaften*, see W. Kalischer, *Die Universität und ihre Studentenschaft* [*The University and Her Students*].

11. Hofstadter and Metzger, *Academic Freedom*, p. 385; Gebhardt, *Humboldt*, p. 114; Lilge, *Abuse*, p. 34.

12. These figures have been reported by Paulsen, *Universitäten*, pp. 101-2, and passed on by others, e.g., Ringer, *Mandarins*, p. 37.

13. The law stated explicitly that ". . . the deliberate promotion of Social Democratic purposes is incompatible with a teaching post in a royal university." R. H. Samuel and R. H. Thomas, *Education and Society in Modern Germany*, p. 117. See also Paulsen, *Universitäten*, pp. 130-1; Ringer, *Mandarins*, p. 55; and Hofstadter and Metzger, *Academic Freedom*, pp. 383-4, 390.

14. Hofstadter and Metzger, *Academic Freedom*, p. 396.

15. This paragraph depends heavily on Metzger's account in Hofstadter and Metzger, *Academic Freedom*, pp. 367-8, 377-8. See also Rudolph, *American College and University*, p. 335.

16. D. Schoenbaum, "The Free University of Berlin, or, How Free Can a University Be?," *AAUP Bulletin*, p. 7.

17. The German university has been well described at the end of the nineteenth century and during the Weimar Republic. The best structural description of the German university at the close of the century is provided by Paulsen, *Universitäten*. The best description of the German university in the Weimar period is Ringer, *Mandarins*, which is also a good source for the turn of the century. There have been a number of articles and books on the German university during the Third Reich. Among the most informative of these are Samuel and Thomas, *Education and Society*; K. O. Aretin, "Die deutsche Universität im dritten Reich" ["The German University in the Third Reich"], *Frankfurter Hefte*; H. Braun, "Die deutsche Universität in den Jahren 1933-1945" ["The German University in the Years Between 1933-1945"], in *Festschrift für Leo Brandt*; E. Y. Hartshorne, *The German Universities and National Socialism*; and G. Ritter, "The German Professor in the Third Reich," *Review of Politics*.

Chapter Six

1. Paulsen, *Universitäten*.

2. Samuel and Thomas, *Education and Society*, p. 164.

3. The "blue brief" and several other important documents treating the matter of university reform in Germany are contained in R. Neuhaus, ed., *Dokumente zur Hochschulreform 1945-1959* [*Documents for Reforming Post-secondary Education 1945-1959*].

4. G. Hess, *Die deutsche Universität 1930-1970* [*The German University 1930-1970*], p. 25.

5. Neuhaus, *Dokumente,* p. 63.

6. G. M. Murch and F. Wesley, "German Psychology and its Journals," *Psychological Bulletin.*

7. W. Bauermeister, *Die berufliche Lage der Nichtordinarien* [*The Occupational Status of the Non-Full Professors*], pp. 40, 54.

8. J. H. Van de Graff, "The Politics of German University Reform, 1810-1970," p. 135. F. Wesley, "Assessing German Psychology—1965," *Journal of General Psychology,* p. 276.

Chapter Seven

1. H. Maier-Leibnitz, "Der Kampf der Wissenschaftler und Bürokraten: Der Filthuth-Prozess oder: Professoren zwischen Forschung, Lehre und Rechnungshof" ["The Battle Between Scientists and Bureaucrats: The Filthuth Case, or, Professors in the Middle Between Research, Teaching, and the Court of Government Auditors"], *Die Zeit.*

2. Dahrendorf, *Society and Democracy.*

3. Meyer-Erlach, "Cultural Scene," p. 173.

4. J. Fijalkowski, "The Structure of German Society after the Second World War," in Payne, *Germany Today.*

5. B. B. Burn, "Higher Education in The Federal Republic of Germany," in Burn, *Higher Education,* p. 171.

6. The consequences of this public-policy change are subtly reflected in the two principal slogans used by the SPD during their reelection campaign in 1972: "We are someone again" (*Wir sind wieder wer*), and "Germans! We can be proud of our country again!" (*Deutsche! Wir können wieder stolz sein auf unser Land!*)

7. The SPD/FDP government declaration of 28 October 1969 states, "Education and training, science and research stand at the head of those reforms which it is appropriate for us to undertake." G. K. Roberts, *West German Politics*, pp. 163-5.

8. Schoenbaum, "Free University of Berlin," p. 7.

9. A good discussion of the concerns leading to the establishment of the *Wissenschaftsrat*, and its early history, is contained in G. Hess and K. Pfuhl, *Wissenschaftsrat 1956-1967*. See also Hess, *deutsche Universität*, pp. 30-2. Because the composition of the *Wissenschaftsrat* virtually guarantees that its members, and thus for the most part its recommendations, tend to reflect the views of established interests, it has been criticized from both the political right, e.g., W. Schöne, *Kampf um die deutsche Universität* [*The Struggle for the German University*]; and the political left, e.g., S. Leibfried, *Die angepasste Universität* [*The Compromised University*], pp. 81-5.

10. The many reports of the *Wissenschaftsrat* continue to be published as a series by J. C. B. Mohr in Tübingen, and provide a valuable historical record of an establishment position on university reform in the Federal Republic. The two reports specifically mentioned in the text are *Empfehlungen zum Ausbau der wissenschaftlichen Einrichtungen* [*Recommendations for the Expansion of Scholarly Institutions*], and *Anregungen zur Gestalt neuer Hochschulen* [*Stimulative Suggestions Toward a Pattern for New Postsecondary Educational Institutions*].

11. R. Wildenmann, "Higher Education in Transition: The Case of the Universities in the Federal Republic of Germany," in S. D. Kertesz, ed., *The Task of Universities in a Changing World*, p. 340.

12. Universität Konstanz, *Die Universität Konstanz: Bericht des Gründungsausschusses* [*The University of Constance: Report of the Founding Committee*].

13. I. N. Sommerkorn, "The Free University of Berlin: Case Study of an Experimental Seminar (1968-69)," in W. R. Niblett and R. F. Butts, eds., *Universities Facing the Future*, p. 336.

14. Bauermeister, *Berufliche Lage*, p. 30.

15. Burn, "Higher Education in the Federal Republic of Germany," p. 175.

16. *Ibid.*, p. 174.

17. Sommerkorn, "Free University of Berlin," p. 336.

18. Schoenbaum, "Free University of Berlin," p. 7.

19. A similar chronology of student unrest in the Federal Republic is contained in Van de Graff, "Politics of German University Reform," pp. 319-23. See also E. Nuissl, R. Rendtorff, and W. D. Webler, *Scheitert die Hochschulreform? [Is University Reform Foundering?]*, pp. 8-29; and Wildenmann, "Higher Education in Transition," p. 338.

20. D. Albers, *Demokratisierung der Hochschule: Argumente zur Drittelparität [Bringing Democracy to the University: Arguments for Triple Parity]*.

21. Some general aspects of the *ausserparlamentarische opposition* (APO), *i.e.*, extraparliamentary opposition, that developed during the period of the Grand Coalition are discussed in Roberts, *West German Politics*, pp. 37, 102, 103, 155, 185.

22. Ringer, *Mandarins*.

23. Nuissl, et al. *Scheitert?*, pp. 30-5. See also E. Becker and G. Jungblut, *Strategien der Bildungsproduktion [Strategies for the Production of Intellect]*.

24. J. Habermas, *Protestbewegung und Hochschulreform* [*The Protest Movement and University Reform*].

25. The most notable exception is H. Schelsky, *Abschied von der Hochschulpolitik* [*Farewell from University Politics*]; and also Schelsky, *Einsamkeit und Freiheit,* pp. 241-68, "Das Ende der Humboldtschen Universität" ["The End of the Humboldtian University"].

26. H. A. Jacobsen and H. Dollinger, *Die deutschen Studenten* [*The German Students*], pp. 202-5.

27. The development of the reform law in the state of Hesse has been carefully described by Van de Graff, "Politics of German University Reform," pp. 232-313, 323-6.

Chapter Eight

1. "Professoren über Professoren: Wieder Elite" [Professors about Professors: Elite Again"], *Der Spiegel,* p. 49, 52.

2. A thorough and informative description of the difficulties in Heidelberg is provided by Nuissl et al., *Scheitert?*

3. For example, W. Brezinka, "German Universities – Crisis and Reform," *Educational Record.*

4. The story of the first years at Constance has been eloquently recounted by G. Hess, *Sieben Jahre Universität Konstanz 1966-1972* [*Seven Years at the University of Constance, 1966-1972*].

5. The triple parity decision of the court is described in H. L. Mason, "Reflections on the Politicized University: 1. The Academic Crisis in the Federal Republic of Germany," *AAUP Bulletin.*

6. "Adorno, Theodor W.," *The New York Times.*

7. The fate of the 1973 draft of the *Hochschulrahmengesetz* is neatly chronicled in a widely-spaced series of articles by H. Matthiesen, an education analyst for the weekly newspaper *Die Zeit:* "Dohnanyis Kampf: ein neues Hochschulrahmengesetz" ["Dohnanyi's Struggle: A New Higher Education Coordinating Law"], (6 July 1973); "Eine Abfuhr fur den Bund" ["A Rebuff for the Government"], (26 Oct. 1973); "Ab ins Grab!" ["Into the Grave!"], (7 Mar. 1975).

8. "Einfach Weggerutscht" ["Simply Pushed Aside"], *Der Spiegel.*

9. A valuable description of the state of the university in the Federal Republic during the early 1970s has been provided by two educational commentators for the weekly newspaper *Die Zeit*, R. W. Leonhardt and N. Grunenberg. In a series of articles, they analyzed the university situation in each of the eleven states of the Federal Republic. These are:

(a) *Hesse.* "Der Student, was möcht er?" ["The Student, What Does He Want?"], 17, (28 Apr. 1972).

(b) *North-Rhine Westphalia.* "Der Minister auf dem Feuerstuhl" ["The Minister on the Hotseat"], (26 Jan. 1973).

(c) *Baden-Württemberg.* "Auf in den Kampf!" ["On into Battle!"], (16 Feb. 1973).

(d) *Lower Saxony.* "Utopist in einem armen Land" ["A Utopian in a Poor Country"], (2 Mar. 1973).

(e) *Bavaria.* "Alle Macht ist oben" ["All Power Flows From Heaven"], (6 Apr. 1973).

(f) *Schleswig-Holstein.* "Kieler Blut. Oder: Wie man Menschen so verbraucht, wie sie sind" ["The Kiel Spirit. Or, How to Use People as You Find Them"], (27 Apr. 1973)

(g) *Bremen.* "Kein Chaos trotz Chaoten" ["No Chaos in Spite of the Crazies"], (18 May 1973).

(h) *Berlin.* "Im Tollhaus an der Spree. Die Ohnmachtsgefühle der Uni-Präsidenten sind verständlich" [In the Madhouse on the

Spree. Those Feelings of Helplessness on the Part of the President of the University are Understandable"], (29 June 1973).

(i) *Rhineland-palatinate*. "Der süsse Friede von Mainz" ["The Sweet Peace of Mainz"], (6 July 1973).

(j) *Saarland*. "Dornröschen an der Saar" ["Sleeping Beauty on the Saar"], (19 Oct. 1973).

(k) *Hamburg*. "Mit hanseatischer Gelassenheit. Liberale Tradition, stille Resignation, ein Krisenkiller als Präsident" ["With Hanseatic Composure. Liberal Tradition, Quiet Resignation, A Crisis Manager as President"], (18 Jan. 1974).

(l) *Summary: Federal Republic*. "Zwischen Revolution und Resignation. Die Reformkrise der deutschen Universität" ["Between Revolution and Resignation. The Reform Crisis of the German University"], (8 Feb. 1974).

10. R. W. Leonhardt, "Zwischen Revolution und Resignation."

11. A full professor was quoted in 1975 as saying, "I have now been a professor for twenty years and I can say that it has never been more fun for me to teach young people. Today, we have the ideal students." R. Reiser, "Anstatt die Welt die Noten verbessern" ["Improving One's Grades Instead of the World"], *Süddeutsche Zeitung*.

12. "Abitur: Einbahnstrasse wird zur Sackgasse" ["Abitur: A One-way Street Turns into a Dead End"], *Der Spiegel*, p. 41.

13. U. Teichler, "Problems of West German Universities on the Way to Mass Higher Education," p. 3.

14. *Ibid.*, pp. 17-18.

15. *Ibid.*, p. 4.

16. Even from a purely administrative point of view, the universities could not cope with the massive numbers of students. Schelsky, *Abschied*, p. 85, claims that in North-Rhine West-

phalia in the late 1960s the reports from the universities of the number of students enrolled differed from the state's statistics by more than 2,000 students per university.

Chapter Nine

1. H. Maier, "15 Jahre Hochschulreform—Gewinn oder Verlust?" ["15 years of university reform: profit or loss?"], *Die deutsche Universitätszeitung vereinigt mit Hochschul-Dienst,* p. 708.

2. "Grober Eingriff" ["Crass Interference"], *Der Spiegel.* "Lauer Ablauf" ["Weak yield"] and "Die Glaubenskriege müssen beendet werden" ["We must stop the crusades"], *Der Spiegel.*

3. R. W. Leonhardt, "Wer soll studieren?" ["Who Shall Study?"], *Die Zeit.* See also H. von Hentig, "Numerus Clausus, Abitur und Alternativen" ["Numerus Clausus, Abitur, and Alternatives"], *Merkur.*

4. Maier, "15 Jahre," states: "No other European nation has a comparable potential for the continued development of science and knowledge and the transmission of these to the next generation," p. 709.

5. E. Böning, "Hochschulreform—Illusion und Wirklichkeit" ["University reform: Illusion and reality"], *Die deutsche Universitätszeitung vereinigt mit Hochschul-Dienst,* p. 399.

WORKS CITED

"Abitur, Einbahnstrasse wird zur Sackgasse." *Der Spiegel*, 26 May 1975, pp. 38-60.

"Adorno, Theodor W." *The New York Times*, 7 August 1969, p. 35.

Albers, D. *Demokratisierung der Hochschule: Argumente zur Drittelparität.* Bonn: Verlag Studentenschaft. 1968.

Anrich, E., ed. *Die Idee der deutschen Universität.* Darmstadt: Wissenschaftliche Buchgesellschaft, 1964.

Aretin, K. O. "Die deutsche Universität im dritten Reich." Frankfurter Hefte 23 (1968): 689-96.

Bauermeister, W. *Die berufliche Lage der Nichtordinarien.* Göttingen: Verlag Otto Schwartz & Co., 1970.

Becker, E., and Jungblut, G. *Strategien der Bildungsproduktion.* Frankfurt am Main: Suhrkamp Verlag, 1972.

Ben-David, J. *Trends in American Higher Education.* Chicago: University of Chicago Press, 1974.

Binswanger, P. *Wilhelm von Humboldt.* Frauenfeld and Leipzig: Huber Verlag, 1937.

Böning, E. "Hochschulreform–Illusion und Wirklichkeit." *Die deutsche Universitätszeitung vereinigt mit Hochschul-Dienst* 13 (1979): 398-402.

Braun, H. "Die deutsche Universität in den Jahren 1933-1945." In *Festschrift für Leo Brandt*, pp. 465-75. Köln and Opladen: Westdeutscher Verlag, 1968.

Brezinka, W. "German Universities—Crisis and Reform." *Educational Record,* Fall (1968): 419-28.

Burn, B. B. "Higher Education in the Federal Republic of Germany." In *Higher Education in Nine Countries,* edited by B. B. Burn, pp. 165-95. New York: McGraw-Hill, 1971.

—————., ed. *Higher Education in Nine Countries.* New York: McGraw-Hill, 1971.

Chomsky, N. *Cartesian Linguistics: A Chapter in the History of Rationalist Thought.* New York: Harper & Row, 1966.

Cross, A. L. "The University of Michigan in Ann Arbor, 1837-1937." In *A University Between Two Centuries,* edited by W. B. Shaw, pp. 49-60. Ann Arbor, Mich.: University of Michigan Press, 1937.

Cubberley, E. P. *The History of Education: Educational Practice and Progress Considered as a Phase of the Development and Spread of Western Civilization.* New York: Houghton Mifflin Co., 1920.

Dahrendorf, R. *Society and Democracy in Germany.* New York: Doubleday, 1967.

DeVane, W. C. *Higher Education in Twentieth Century America.* Cambridge: Harvard University Press, 1965.

"Einfach Weggerutscht." *Der Spiegel,* 15 December 1975, pp. 26-7.

Farrand, M. *The Framing of the Constitution of the United States.* New Haven: Yale University Press, 1913.

Fichte, J. G. "Deduzierter Plan einer in Berlin zu errichtenden höheren Lehranstalt." In *Die Idee der deutschen Universität,* edited by E. Anrich, pp. 124-218. Darmstadt: Wissenschaftliche Gesellschaft, 1964.

Fijalkowski, J. "The Structure of German Society after the Second World War." In *Germany Today: Introductory Studies,* edited by J. P. Payne, pp. 84-110. London: Methuen & Co., 1971.

Flexner, A. *Universities: American, English, German.* New York: Oxford University Press, 1930.

Fried, A., ed. *The Essential Jefferson.* New York: Collier Books, 1963.

Gebhardt, B. *Wilhelm von Humboldt als Staatsmann. Bd. I.* 1896. Reprint. Aalen: Scientia Verlag, 1965.

Giese, G. *Quellen zur deutschen Schulgeschichte seit 1800.* Göttingen: Musterschmidt, 1961.

"Die Glaubenskriege müssen beendet werden." *Der Spiegel,* 9 July 1979, pp. 79-80.

Good, H. G., and Teller, J. D. *A History of Western Education.* 3rd ed. New York: MacMillan, 1969.

"Grober Eingriff." *Der Spiegel,* 30 April 1979, pp. 89-91.

Grunenberg, N. "Der Minister auf dem Feuerstuhl." *Die Zeit,* 26 January 1973, pp. 11-12.

—————. "Utopist in einem armen Land." *Die Zeit,* 2 March 1973, pp. 19-20.

—————. "Alle Macht ist oben." *Die Zeit,* 6 April 1973, pp. 20-21.

—————. "Kieler Blut. Oder: Wie man Menschen so verbraucht, wie sie sind." *Die Zeit,* 27 April 1973, pp. 17-18.

—————. "Im Tollhaus an der Spree. Die Ohnmachtsgefühle der Uni-Präsidenten sind verständlich." *Die Zeit,* 29 June 1973, pp. 17-18.

—————. "Mit hanseatischer Gelassenheit. Liberale Tradition, stille Resignation, ein Krisenkiller als Präsident." *Die Zeit,* 18 January 1974, pp. 16-17.

Habermas, J. *Protestbewegung und Hochschulreform.* Frankfurt am Main: Suhrkamp Verlag, 1969.

Hahne, H. "Gegenwart im Dasein: Wilhelm von Humboldt, geboren am 22. Juni 1767." *Frankfurter allgemeine Zeitung,* 16-17 June 1967.

Hall, G. S. "Educational Reforms." *The Pedagogical Seminary,* now *Journal of Genetic Psychology* 1 (1891): 1-12.

Hartshorne, E. Y. *The German Universities and National Socialism.* London: George Allen & Unwin, 1937.

Hearndon, A. *Education in the Two Germanies.* Boulder, Colo.: Westview Press, 1976.

Hentig, H. von. "Numerus Clausus, Abitur und Alternativen." *Merkur* 315 (1974): 905-21; 316 (1974): 1015-33.

Hess, G. *Die deutsche Universität 1930-1970.* Bad Godesberg: Inter Nationes, 1968.

————. *Sieben Jahre Universität Konstanz 1966-1972.* Konstanz: Universitätsverlag, 1973.

Hess, G., and Pfuhl, K. *Wissenschaftsrat 1957-1967.* Tübingen: J. C. B. Mohr, 1968.

Hofstadter, R., and Metzger, W. P. *The Development of Academic Freedom in the United States.* New York: Columbia University Press, 1955.

Humboldt, W. von. "Über die innere und äussere Organization der höheren wissenschaftlichen Anstalten zu Berlin." In *Die Idee der deutschen Universität,* edited by E. Anrich, pp. 375-86. Darmstadt: Wissenschaftliches Gesellschaft, 1964.

Jacobsen, H. A., and Dollinger, H. *Die deutschen Studenten.* Munich: Bestandsaufnahme, 1968.

Kalischer, W. *Die Universität und ihre Studentenschaft.* Essen-Bredeny: Stiftverband für die deutsche Wissenschaft, 1966.

Kerr, C. "Introduction: The Evaluation of National Systems of Higher Education." In *Higher Education in Nine Countries,* edited by B. B. Burn, pp. 1-6. New York: McGraw-Hill, 1971.

Kertesz, S. D., ed. *The Task of Universities in a Changing World.* Notre Dame, Ind.: Notre Dame University Press, 1971.

Knoll, J. H. "Vater der Universität: Zum 200. Geburtstag Wilhelm v. Humboldts." *Die Welt,* 16-17 June 1967.

König, R. *Vom Wesen der deutschen Universität: Mit einem Vorwort zum Neudruck.* Darmstadt: Wissenschaftliche Buchgesellschaft, 1970.

Krüsi, H. *Pestalozzi: His Life, Work, and Influence.* New York: Wilson, Hinkle & Co., 1875.

"Lauer Ablauf." *Der Spiegel,* 9 July 1979, p. 79.

Leibfried, S. *Die angepasste Universität.* Frankfurt am Main: Suhrkamp Verlag, 1968.

Lenz, M. *Geschichte der königlichen Friedrich-Wilhelms-Universität zu Berlin. Bd. I.* Halle: Verlag der Buchhandlung des Waisenhauses, 1910.

Leonhardt, R. W. "Der Student, was möcht er?" *Die Zeit,* 28 April 1972, pp. 13-14.

————. "Auf in den Kampf!" *Die Zeit,* 16 February 1973, pp. 15-16.

————. "Kein Chaos trotz Chaoten." *Die Zeit,* 18 May 1973, pp. 17-18.

————. "Der süsse Friede von Mainz." *Die Zeit,* 6 July 1973, pp. 17-18.

————. "Dornröschen an der Saar." *Die Zeit,* 19 October 1973, pp. 17-18.

————. "Zwischen Revolution und Resignation. Die Reformkrise der deutschen Universität." *Die Zeit,* 8 February 1974, pp. 17-18.

————. "Wer soll studieren?" *Die Zeit,* 12 July 1974, p. 1.

Lilge, F. *The Abuse of Learning: The Failure of the German University.* New York: MacMillan, 1948.

Lübbe, H. "Mythos oder Modell? Humboldts preussische Universitätsreform." *Hamburger Sonntagsblatt,* 18 June 1967.

Maier, H. "15 Jahre Hochschulreform — Gewinn oder Verlust?" *Die deutsche Universitätszeitung vereinigt mit Hochschul-Dienst* 22 (1979): 706-9.

Maier-Leibnitz, H. "Der Kampf der Wissenschaftler und Bürokraten: Der Filthuth-Prozess oder: Professoren zwischen Forschung, Lehre und Rechnungshof." *Die Zeit,* 4 January 1974, p. 13.

Mason, H. L. "Reflections on the Politicized University: 1. The Academic Crisis in the Federal Republic of Germany." *AAUP Bulletin* 60 (1974): 299-312.

Matthiesen, H. "Dohnanyis Kampf: ein neues Hochschulrahmengesetz." *Die Zeit,* 6 July 1973, p. 18.

————. "Eine Abfuhr für den Bund." *Die Zeit,* 26 October 1973, p. 17.

————. "Ab ins Grab!" *Die Zeit,* 7 March 1975, p. 10.

Meyer-Erlach, W. "The Cultural Scene in Germany Today." In *Germany Today: Introductory Studies,* edited by J. P. Payne, pp. 153-78. London: Methuen, 1971.

Moore-Rinvolucri, M. J. *Education in East Germany.* Hamden, Conn.: Archon Books, 1973.

Murch, G. M., and Wesley, F. "German Psychology and its Journals." *Psychological Bulletin* 66(1966): 410-15.

Neuhaus, R., ed. *Dokumente zur Hochschulreform 1945-1959.* Wiesbaden: Steiner Verlag, 1961.

Niblett, W. R., and Butts, R. F., eds. *Universities Facing the Future.* San Francisco: Jossey-Bass, 1972.

Nuissl, E., Rendtorff, R.; and Webler, W.-D. *Scheitert die Hochschulreform?* Reinbek bei Hamburg: Rowohlt Taschenbuch Verlag, 1973.

Paulsen, F. *Die deutschen Universitäten und das Universitätsstudium.* 1902. Reprint. Hildesheim: Georg Olms Verlagsbuchhandlung, 1966.

_____. *The German Universities and University Study.* Translated by F. Thilly and W. W. Elang. New York: C. Scribner's Sons, 1906.

_____. *Geschichte des gelehrten Unterrichts. Erster Band.* Leipzig: Verlag von Veit, 1919.

_____. *Geschichte des gelehrten Unterrichts. Zweiter Band.* Berlin and Leipzig: Walter de Gruyten & Co., 1921.

Payne, J. P., ed. *Germany Today: Introductory Studies.* London: Methuen, 1971.

"Professoren über Professoren: Wieder Elite." *Der Spiegel,* 6 January 1975, pp. 46-52.

Reiser, R. "Anstatt die Welt die Noten verbessern." *Süddeutsche Zeitung,* 21-22 June 1975, pp. 15-16.

Ringer, F. K. *The Decline of the German Mandarins.* Cambridge: Harvard University Press, 1969.

Ritter, G. "The German Professor in the Third Reich." *Review of Politics* 8 (1946): 242-54.

Roberts, G. K. *West German Politics.* New York: Taplinger Publishing Co., 1972.

Rothfels, H., ed. *Berlin in Vergangenheit und Gegenwart, Tübinger Vorträge.* Tübingen: J. C. B. Mohr, Paul Siebeck, 1961.

Rudolph, F. *The American College and University: A History.* New York: Knopf, 1962.

Samuel, R. H., and Thomas, R. H. *Education and Society in Modern Germany.* 1949. Reprint. Westport, Conn.: Greenwood Press, 1971.

Schelsky, H. *Abschied von der Hochschulpolitik.* Bielefeld: Bertelsmann Universitätsverlag, 1969.

—————. *Einsamkeit und Freiheit: Idee und Gestalt der deutschen Universität und ihrer Reformen. 2., um einen "Nachtrag, 1970" erweiterte Auflage.* Düsseldorf: Bertelsmann Universitätsverlag, 1971.

Schleiermacher, F. E. D. "Gelegentliche Gedanken über Universitäten im deutschen Sinn." In *Die Idee der deutschen Universität,* edited by E. Anrich, pp. 219-308. Darmstadt: Wissenschaftliche Buchgesellschaft, 1964.

Schoenbaum, D. "The Free University of Berlin, or, How Free Can a University Be?" *AAUP Bulletin* 59 (1973): 5-9.

Schöne, W. *Kampf um die deutsche Universität.* Hamburg, Selbstverlag, 1966.

Schurtz, S. B. "The First Twenty Years." In *A University Between Two Centuries,* edited by W. B. Shaw, pp. 35-45. Ann Arbor, Mich.: University of Michigan Press, 1937.

Shaw, W. B., ed. *A University Between Two Centuries.* Ann Arbor, Mich.: University of Michigan Press, 1937.

Slosson, E. E. *Great American Universities.* New York: MacMillan, 1910.

Sommerkorn, I. N. "The Free University of Berlin: Case Study of an Experimental Seminar (1968-69)." In *Universities Facing the Future,* edited by W. R. Niblett and R. F. Butts, pp. 336-46. San Francisco: Jossey Bass, 1972.

Sörgel, W. *Befragung von Lehrenden an Hochschulen, Sommersemester 1974.* Munich: Münchner Infratest Institut, 1974.

Spranger, E. *Wilhelm von Humboldt und die Humanitätsidee.* Berlin: Reuther & Reichard, 1909.

——————. *Wilhelm von Humboldt und die Reform des Bildungs-wesens.* Berlin: Reuther & Reichard, 1910.

——————. "Mein Konflikt mit der national-sozialistischen Reigierung 1933." *Universitas: Zeitschrift für Wissenschaft, Kunst und Literator* 10 (1955): 457-73.

——————. "Gedenkrede zur 150–Jahrfeier der Gründung der Friedrich-Wilhelms Universität in Berlin." In *Berlin in Vergangenheit und Gegenwart, Tübinger Vorträge,* edited by H. Rothfels, pp. 61-74. Tübingen: J. C. B. Mohr, Paul Siebeck, 1961.

Stone, L., ed. *The University in Society.* Vol. 2. Princeton: Princeton University Press, 1974.

Teichler, U. "Problems of West German Universities on the Way to Mass Higher Education." Mimeographed Conference Paper. Berlin: Max-Planck-Institut für Bildungsforschung, 1975.

Turner, R. S. "University Reformers and Professorial Scholarship in Germany 1760-1806." In *The University in Society,* edited by L. Stone, pp. 495-531. Princeton: Princeton University Press, 1974.

Universität Konstanz. *Die Universität Konstanz: Bericht des Gründungsausschusses.* Konstanz: Universitätsverlag, 1965.

Van de Graff, J. H. "The Politics of German University Reform, 1810-1970." Ph.D. dissertation. Columbia University, 1973.

Walther, H. "Die Revolution des Jahres 1848 und die Reform der Universitäten in Deutschland." *Freiburger Universitäts-blätter* 9 (1970): 19-27.

Wesley, F. "Assessing German Psychology–1965." *The Journal of General Psychology* 75 (1966): 273-7.

Wildenmann, R. "Higher Education in Transition: The Case of the Universities in the Federal Republic of Germany." In *The Task of Universities in a Changing World,* edited by S. D. Kertesz, pp. 336-52. Notre Dame, Ind.: Notre Dame University Press, 1971.

Wirzberger, K. H. *Die Humboldt-Universität zu Berlin: Bilder aus Vergangenheit und Gegenwart.* East Berlin: VEB Deutscher Verlag der Wissenschaften, 1973.

Wissenschaftsrat. *Empfehlungen zum Ausbau der wissenschaftlichen Einrichtungen. Teil I: Wissenschaftliche Hochschulen.* Tübingen: J. C. B. Mohr, 1960.

—————. *Anregungen zur Gestalt neuer Hochschulen.* Tübingen: J. C. B. Mohr, 1962.

Index

Abitur: emergence as principal qualifying examination, 18-19, 19*n*; and *Numerus Clausus,* 96-97; West German Conference of University Rectors proposes abolishment, 102

Academic degrees: in nineteenth century German university, 38-40; Ph.D., 52

Academic freedom: *Lehrfreiheit,* the freedom to teach, and *Lernfreiheit,* the freedom to learn, 28; protected in German national constitutions, 29; first clearly enunciated at Halle, 29; examples of violations of in nineteenth-century Germany, 46*n*, 48-50, 114*n13*; influence on the United States of German respect for, 50-51; and University of Constance, 88

Academic ranks: comparison of German and American, 33, 43-44, 112*n2*

Adenauer, Konrad, 73

Adorno, Theodor Weisengrund, 78, 89

Altenstein, Karl vom Stein zum, 13

American Association of University Professors, 50*n*

American higher education:

influenced by the German university, 1-3, 51-52, 105*n1*; private vs. public distinction, 22-23; origin of the Ph.D. degree, 52; as model for German university, 56; German university described for American audience in 1966, 58

American Psychological Association, 2

Arons, Leo, 50

Arts and sciences: freed from domination by "higher" faculties, 29-30

Association for Academic Freedom: 81-82, 82*n*

Association of Democratic Scholars, 82*n*

Augsburg, University of, 95

Ausserordentlicher Professor, 44. *See also* Academic ranks

Austrian universities, 4*n*

Bad Honnef conference, 65

Beethoven, Ludwig van, 14

Below, Georg von, 46*n*

Berlin, Free University of: established, 11; student protest, 73-74; mentioned as example, 95

Berlin, University of: after 1945, 4*n*, 11, 55, 108*n3*; intellectual climate at founding, 14; physical setting,

University of Constance, 71,
83, 84; struggles to negotiate
compromise, 86-87; resigns
as rector, 87

Hinterzarten, conference, 65-66

Hochschulrahmengesetz. See Federal coordinating law

Humboldt, Alexander von, 14

Humboldt, Friedrich Wilhelm
Christian Karl Ferdinand,
Freiherr von. *See* Humboldt,
Wilhelm von

Humboldt, Friedrich Wilhelm
Karl Heinrich Alexander,
Freiherr von. *See* Humboldt,
Alexander von

Humboldt University of
Berlin, 11. *See also* University of Berlin, German
Democratic Republic

Humboldt, Wilhelm von:
arrives in Berlin (1808), 9;
father of the university, 10;
role in establishing the University of Berlin, 11, 12-14,
109*n7*; memorandum on
concept of a university, 11,
30, 108*n5*; praised by
German Democratic Republic, 11, 108*n3*; reluctant to
accept ministry post in
Berlin, 11-12; disagreement
with Hardenberg, 13; career
and family, 13, 14-15; interest in antiquity and linguistics, 15, 15*n*, 109*n11*;
reforms elementary and secondary education in Prussia,
15-19; views on methods of
Pestalozzi, 16-17; establishes

Gymnasium, 17-18; views on
faculty, 19-21, 25-26; names
the University of Berlin,
20*n*, 30-31, 108*n3*; views on
relation between university
and state, 21-25; three principles basic to the university, 28-29; establishes
commission to draft statutes
for new University of
Berlin, 32; argues for special
faculty qualifying examination, 41; mentioned, 50-60
passim, 81, 88, 98, 99

Humboldtian university. *See*
German university

Idealism, in German philosophy, 7

Institute for Advanced Study
(Princeton), 3

Jahn, Gerhard, 92

Jefferson, Thomas, 23

Jena, University of: influenced
by enlightenment, 6, 7, 8;
reputation helps name of
University, 30

Johns Hopkins University:
influenced by German university, 1; first U.S. graduate
school, 2; staff at opening
described, 52

Karlsruhe, Technical University of, 91

Kennedy, John Fitzgerald, 72

Kerr, Clark, 3

Kiesinger, Kurt Georg: leader
in founding University of

ABOUT THE AUTHOR

DANIEL FALLON was born in Colombia, South America, and was educated in the United States at Antioch College, where he received his B.A., and at the University of Virginia, where he received his M.A. and Ph.D. degrees. Professor of Psychology and Dean of the College of Liberal Arts and Sciences at the University of Colorado at Denver, Fallon is an experimental psychologist with specialization in learning and motivation. Before coming to Colorado he was employed by the State University of New York at Binghamton, where he taught psychology, performed research, and was active in academic administration. His interest in the German university stems from several years he spent as both student and teacher at German universities.